MAKING CHOICES:

Life Skills for Adolescents

WORKBOOK

By Mary Halter and Barbara Fierro Lang

Advocacy Press, Santa Barbara, California

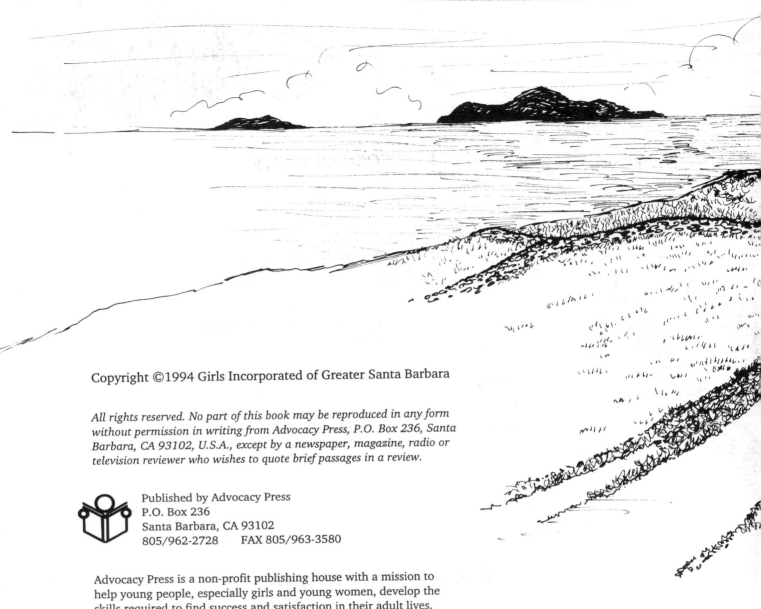

Published by Advocacy Press
P.O. Box 236
Santa Barbara, CA 93102
805/962-2728   FAX 805/963-3580

Advocacy Press is a non-profit publishing house with a mission to help young people, especially girls and young women, develop the skills required to find success and satisfaction in their adult lives. Advocacy Press is a Division of Girls Incorporated of Greater Santa Barbara, an affiliate of Girls Incorporated.

10   9   8

Manufactured in the United States of America

Front Cover Design and Art: Robert Howard
Book Design and Typography: Cirrus Design

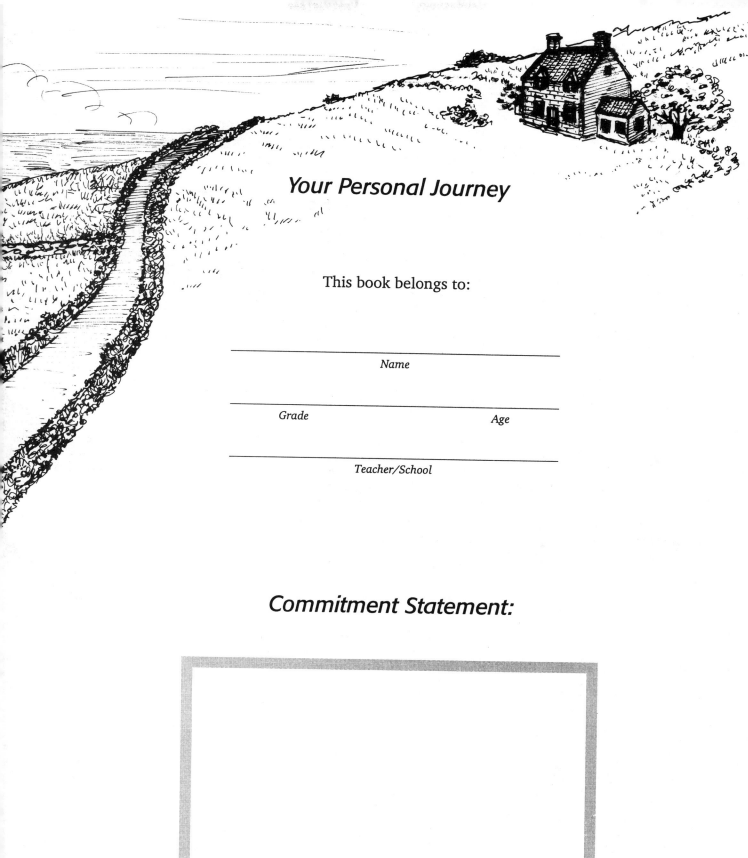

Your Personal Journey

This book belongs to:

_____

Name

_____

Grade   *Age*

_____

Teacher/School

Commitment Statement:

CONTENTS

Foreword

This course is designed to be a personal journey for you. By participating, you will learn the importance of acquiring certain skills so you can be the successful navigator of your own life.

If you were the captain of a sailing vessel setting out to sea, you would need to know about the ocean and its inhabitants. You'd have to learn how to sail the boat, map your course, operate the instruments and equipment and choose the right people to travel with. You'd want to be able to insure the safety of your craft and crew, get your supplies, know what the dangers are and be ready for emergencies. You'd have to know how to work and live cooperatively with the other people on the boat. If you prepare well, chances are you would choose an exciting destination and enjoy your trip. You'd know how to make the right choices for *you* and for those who trust you.

You probably wouldn't even think about setting out to sea until you learned what you needed to know. Life is a journey, too. In order to have the life style you would like, will you take the time to prepare for it just as carefully as you would prepare to become the captain of a boat?

For generations, people have not prepared well for some of their most important journeys. Most people, even those who go to college and graduate, are not well prepared for some of their most important responsibilities. They have children, work at jobs, choose mates, leave home, buy cars, set up housing, and move from place to place.

Most of what we learn about living our life is by "osmosis." In other words, we pick it up as we go. It's not a conscious learning process. But, this isn't always the best way to learn. We sometimes learn things that hurt us rather than help us. And sometimes there are gaps in what we learn.

We hope by taking this course you will learn about some of the skills you will need as you grow older. You are the navigator of your life—you are **MAKING CHOICES**.

Introduction

LESSON ONE — Understanding the Course

There are five parts to *Making Choices*. The first part, **Appreciating Differences**, helps to give you a broader understanding of the world around you.

The second book, **Personal Development**, helps you understand how you develop as a human being.

The third book, **Family and Values**, helps you get to know yourself and understand how the people and experiences in your life have influenced your choice making. It helps you understand the importance of being healthy and fit. Here you will identify some of the skills you will need to be a successful navigator.

The fourth book, *Making Choices*, helps you learn to decide where you want to go and how to map your course. You will also learn to calculate the cost of your journey.

In the fifth book, **Making a Difference**, you will discover how you can solve the problems that come up and help make the world a better place.

Are you ready? Let's GO!

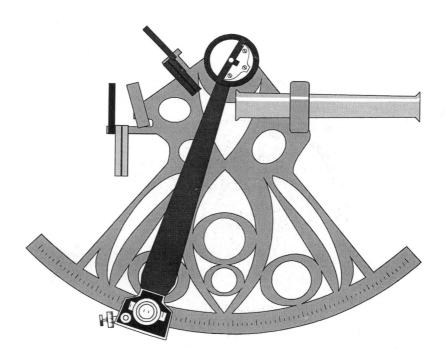

Throughout our course we will adhere to the following Ground Rules. If your class adds other ground rules that everyone agrees upon, add them to the list.

GROUND RULES

- ◆ Be respectful of other people's opinions.
- ◆ Value everyone's ideas—they are important!
- ◆ Don't interrupt.
- ◆ There are no dumb questions.
- ◆ It's OK to pass (not participate if you're uncomfortable).
- ◆ There are no put-downs.
- ◆ Everything that anyone shares in our class is confidential.

- ◆ _____
- ◆ _____
- ◆ _____
- ◆ _____
- ◆ _____
- ◆ _____
- ◆ _____
- ◆ _____
- ◆ _____

You will need to make the following commitments to be ready for this personal journey. If your class adds others that everyone agrees upon, add them to the list below:

WHAT YOU NEED TO BE READY

- ◆ Be on time for class.
- ◆ Be enthusiastic.
- ◆ Have a good attitude.
- ◆ Be prepared.
- ◆ Bring necessary materials.
- ◆ Have a commitment to learn.
- ◆ Be open to new ideas.

- ◆ _____
- ◆ _____
- ◆ _____
- ◆ _____
- ◆ _____
- ◆ _____
- ◆ _____
- ◆ _____
- ◆ _____

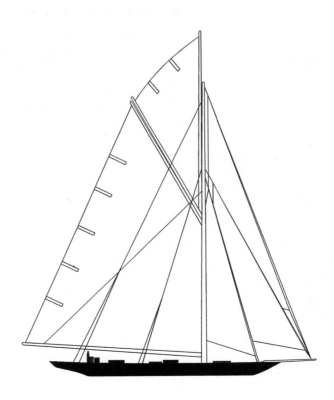

LESSON TWO — Friday Forums

Friday Forums

Objective: You will take part in student-directed forums which give you an opportunity to utilize some of the skills you are developing.

Topics:

◆ THE WORLD TODAY
- Politics
  - Local
  - National
- Environmental Issues
- Hunger
- Economy/Employment
- Foreign Relations

◆ TEEN HEALTH ISSUES
- Mental Health
- Access to Health Care
- School-based Clinics
- Nutrition
- STDs/HIV

◆ TEENS AND VIOLENCE
- Gun Control
- Gang Relations
- Juvenile Justice
- Date Violence
- Domestic Violence
- Sexual Assault

◆ CRIME PREVENTION
- Community Service
- Block Watch
- Volunteer Patrols
- Resource Officer at School
- Peer Support Groups
- "Safe Rides" (Students Without Transportation)
- Campus Security
- Peer Leadership Training
- Closed/Open Campuses

◆ TEEN PREGNANCY AND PARENTING
- Continuing Education
- Child Care
- Parenting Classes
- Sexuality Education
- Health Care

◆ PREJUDICE REDUCTION
- Cultural Sensitivity
- Cultural Learning Opportunities
- Conflict Resolution

◆ SUBSTANCE ABUSE

◆ SOCIAL ACTION
- People Making a Difference
  - Youth
  - Adults
- Projects Where We Can Make a Difference

During this course we will have **Friday Forums** on most Fridays. Some Fridays will be reserved for special classes or guest speakers. Some Fridays will be used as an opportunity to complete a lesson or lessons if we are not on schedule. *Most* Fridays will be reserved for the class to plan. You will choose the category and the topic for the day.

Use this worksheet to help you and/or your team plan for your day.

FRIDAY FORUM CATEGORY: _____

TOPIC: _____

DATE OF PRESENTATION: _____

TEAM MEMBERS: _____

RESOURCES NEEDED:	SECURED FROM:	WHEN:
	_____	_____
	_____	_____
	_____	_____

ACTION STEPS:	BY WHOM:	WHEN:
	_____	_____
	_____	_____
	_____	_____

BOOK ONE
Appreciating Differences

CHAPTER ONE — GENDER EQUITY

LESSON ONE — Recognizing Gender Bias

Student Career Survey

The survey below will help you learn how you feel about career and work. Please respond to each statement by checking the answer that best describes how you feel.

	Agree	Disagree	Not sure
SCHOOL SECTION			
1. In our school, teachers treat boys and girls the same way.			
2. Teachers help me consider many different career choices, including those that are non-traditional.			
3. In our school, there are courses that are clearly "boys' courses" and "girls' courses."			
4. Teachers expect the same thing from girls and boys.			
5. In my classes, boys and girls are placed in separate groups for activities or projects.			
6. I believe I have the right to enroll in any course in the school.			
I will plan my high school classes based on:			
7. my interests			
8. what I am good at			
9. what my friends are taking			
10. what I need for college			
11. what I need for a career			
In school, I am encouraged to do good work in:			
12. math			
13. science			
14. reading			

	Agree	Disagree	Not sure
15. Doing good work in school is important to me.			
16. Doing good work in school will help me prepare for my career.			

WORK SECTION

	Agree	Disagree	Not sure
17. Most women work because they need the money.			
18. Most people living below the poverty level are women and their children.			
19. Women and men should be trained to get good jobs.			
20. Nine out of ten women work for pay sometime during their lives.			
21. Most men work because they need the money.			
22. Women make up 8% (two out of 25) of the engineers in the United States.			
23. Engineers make an average annual salary of $49,200.			
24. 99% of all secretaries are women.			
25. Secretaries earn average annual salaries of $24,000.			
26. Overall, women make 75 cents for every dollar men make.			
27. "Women's jobs" and "men's jobs" are becoming a thing of the past.			

FAMILY SECTION

	Agree	Disagree	Not sure
28. Today, more and more children live in homes with just one parent.			
29. I learn about different careers from watching TV.			
30. In our family, males and females share jobs at home.			
31. I plan to have a career.			
32. I plan to have a family and a career.			
33. In most families, both parents work at jobs outside the home.			

	Agree	Disagree	Not sure
SELF-AWARENESS SECTION			
34. I would like to find out more about possible careers.			
35. The career I choose is important to my parents.			
36. I feel good about myself.			
37. I feel I could be whatever I want to be when I grow up.			
38. How I feel about myself affects how well I do.			
39. I enjoy learning to do new things.			
40. I feel that I am good at many things.			
41. My parents would support my career choice.			

I plan to get help in planning my career from:

	Agree	Disagree	Not sure
42. parents			
43. teachers			
44. school counselors			
45. other people I know			

This exercise adapted from the "Wisconsin Model for Sex Equity in Career and Vocational Education," Wisconsin Department of Public Instruction, 1990, pp. 202-203, printed with permission.

LESSON TWO — Personalizing Gender Bias

After watching the video or the skit presented by students, complete your answers to the following questions:

1. What was your reaction to the presentation and why?

_____

_____

2. How did you feel about the comments the boys were making?

_____

_____

3. Did you become aware that the comments were actually made by girls before it ended and if so, when?

_____

_____

4. Do you think the girls in our class would react the same way? Why or why not?

_____

_____

5. Did the comments made seem realistic to you? Why or why not?

_____

_____

6. Think of an example of gender bias in your own life and be prepared to discuss it in class.

_____

_____

LESSON THREE — Gender Bias and Politics

Women have not always had the same rights as men. Below are some facts about actions which took place during the past fifty years that provided more rights for women in the workplace and in government.

♦ 1941—President Franklin D. Roosevelt prohibits racial discrimination by defense contractors at the start of World War II. Women fill jobs vacated by men who have gone to war.

♦ 1945-1960—Postwar nostalgia for the joys of family life and pressure to make room in the job market for returning GIs send millions of working women home. The housewife is glorified, while tradition and protective legislation keep women out of high-paying "men's jobs."

♦ 1961—As the civil rights movement spreads, President John F. Kennedy's Executive Order 10925 mandates federal contractors to take "affirmative action" to ensure that there be no discrimination by race, creed, color or national origin— in employment, upgrading, demotion, transfer, recruitment, recruitment advertising, layoff, pay and other compensation and selection for training, including apprenticeships. Kennedy also establishes the President's Committee on Equal Employment Opportunity, chaired by the vice president, to help employers promote nondiscrimination.

♦ 1963—Congress passes the Equal Pay Act, which forbids employers to pay women less than men for the same work (defined as jobs with equal skill, effort, responsibility).

♦ 1964—Congress passes the Civil Rights Act. Title VII of the act bans employment discrimination based on race, color, religion, sex or national origin and creates the Equal Employment Opportunity Commission (EEOC) to enforce Title VII and other anti-discrimination laws.

♦ 1965 President Lyndon B. Johnson's Executive Order 11246 requires federal contractors to take "affirmative action" to recruit, hire and promote more minorities among their 21 million employees. It raises the threat of contractors being barred from future government work if they fail to comply.

♦ 1965—President Johnson replaces the President's Committee on Equal Employment Opportunity with the Office of Federal Contract Compliance (OFCC), a Labor Department watchdog on the actions of federal contractors.

♦ 1967—President Johnson adds women to the groups protected under his previous order by issuing Executive Order 11375.

♦ 1967—Congress passes the Age Discrimination in Employment Act, which protects employees between 40 and 70 from discrimination in hiring, firing and other terms of employment.

- 1971—President Richard M. Nixon's Revised Order No. 4 strengthens the two Johnson executive orders to require annual written affirmative-action plans from major contractors. It establishes goals and timetables as the benchmark measures of employers' affirmative-action activities.

- 1971—House approves Women's Equal Rights Amendment (ERA).

- 1972—Title IX of the Educational Amendments of 1972 bars sex bias in institutions receiving any federal money. Originally it was interpreted to mean that if any part of an institution received money, the whole institution was held to this standard. (The 1984 Grove City Supreme Court case limits Title IX programs to cover only the "program or activity" that received the federal funds.)

- 1973—The Rehabilitation Act forbids discrimination against qualified individuals with handicaps who can perform the essential functions of the job with "reasonable accommodation."

- 1975—President Gerald Ford reorganizes the OFCC as the OFCCP (Office of Federal Contract Compliance Programs) to include protection of two more minority groups: handicapped workers and Vietnam War veterans.

- 1978—The Pregnancy Discrimination Act extends the protection of Title VII to pregnant employees. This means, for instance, that pregnant employees cannot be denied disability insurance payments given to other workers with temporary disabilities.

- 1979—President Jimmy Carter organizes and strengthens enforcement of civil rights laws. He unifies enforcement of Title VII, the Equal Pay Act, Age Discrimination Act and Rehabilitation Act under the EEOC. He also transfers enforcement of all federal-contract compliance programs from the individual contracting agencies (the Defense Department, for example) to a single OFCCP office in the Labor Department.

- 1981—Sandra Day O'Connor is appointed to the Supreme Court.

- 1982—ERA lapses without ratification.

- 1983—Sally Ride is the first female astronaut to travel in space.

- 1983—Washington State is ordered to pay female employees according to "comparable worth."

- 1983—President Ronald Reagan signs Executive Order 12432 requiring federal agencies to increase their goals for employment of minority-owned subcontractors by at least 10 percent. Meanwhile other Reagan administration officials argue that all such "quotas" are illegal.

- 1984—Geraldine Ferraro wins the nomination of the Democratic Party as its candidate for vice president.

- 1985—The Reagan administration considers repealing affirmative action requirements for federal contractors, in place for 20 years. It says the rules are costly and encourage discrimination against whites without helping blacks.

- 1986—In two landmark cases the Supreme Court reaffirms the use of affirmative action.

♦ 1992—Women's groups form Women In Senate and House (Republicans) and Emily's List (Democrats) to back female candidates for political office.

♦ 1992—California is the first state to elect two women to serve in the Senate. They are Diane Feinstein and Barbara Boxer.

♦ 1993—President Clinton appoints Janet Reno as the first female U.S. Attorney General.

Now record current information about the following women in politics:

Names/dates of female nominees for Supreme Court and members of Supreme Court

_____

_____

Names/dates of female nominees and appointees to cabinet posts

_____

_____

Names/dates of current and past females who have been elected governor of their state

_____

_____

Percentage of national population which represents women

_____

_____

Percentage of representation by women this year in

Senate _____

House _____

State and local elected and appointed positions held by women

_____

_____

INSTRUCTIONS:

Using a long piece of butcher paper, arrange the above events on a time line in chronological order. This may be assigned as a class project and the time line could be hung in the classroom for everyone to see and discuss.

LESSON FOUR — Wealth, Poverty and Glass Ceiling Jobs

Gender/Salary Test

Think about the working adults you know and what each male or female does for a living. Think about places you see people working. Are most of the teachers in your school male or female? How many female doctors have you seen compared to the male doctors you've seen? What about construction sites? Are there more men or women working there?

Listed below are several occupations. If there were 100 workers in each occupation, how many do you think would be men? How many would be women? The total (male + female) for any one occupation should not exceed 100. The number you enter on each line is a *percentage*. Do not enter anything in the third column for now.

	Female	Male	
Architect	%	%	$
Telephone Installer	%	%	$
Engineer	%	%	$
Date Entry Clerk	%	%	$
Bookkeeper	%	%	$
Accountant	%	%	$
Computer Programmer	%	%	$
Secretary	%	%	$
Dental Assistant	%	%	$
Bank Teller	%	%	$
Dentist	%	%	$
General Practice Physician	%	%	$
Surgeon	%	%	$
Lawyer	%	%	$
Mail Carrier	%	%	$
Nurse	%	%	$
Elementary School Teacher	%	%	$
Electrician	%	%	$
Painter	%	%	$
Carpenter	%	%	$
Air Traffic Controller	%	%	$
Airplane Mechanic	%	%	$
Pilot	%	%	$
Flight Attendant	%	%	$
Truck Driver (Long Distance)	%	%	$
Plumber	%	%	$
Receptionist	%	%	$
Retail Clerk	%	%	$

Now that you have estimated the percentages, fill in the third column by listing the average salary for each occupation. National averages from the *Occupational Outlook Handbook* are provided below. However, try to research the salaries that are paid for these occupations in *your community* before you use these for your answer. That way, you will have a clearer idea of what your local economy is like. You may be able to get this information from the classified ads in your newspaper or from job listings at local employment offices.

Accountant	$ 21,108	Carpenter	27,100
Architect	36,100	Painter	27,100
Telephone Installer	34,100	Plumber	27,000
Engineer	49,200	Air Traffic Controller	31,600
Data Entry Clerk	20,800	Airplane Mechanic	80,000
Bookkeeper	19,100	Pilot	27,200
Secretary	24,100	Flight Attendant	30,000
Computer Programmer	27,060	Truck Driver (Long Distance)	34,400
Dentist	125,700	Nurse	34,400
Dental Assistant	17,300	Physican	155,800
Bank Teller	14,800	Surgeon	250,000 +
Lawyer	120,000	Receptionist	16,100
Mail Carrier	31,300	Retail Clerk	13,000
Elementary School Teacher	32,400		
Electrician	28,600		

Study your answers. Which occupations earn the most?

_____

Look at the salaries of the jobs in which the *percentage* is higher for *men* than for women.

_____

Now look at the salaries of the jobs in which the *percentage* is higher for *women* than for men.

_____

Who earns more money, men or women?

_____

This exercise is adapted from *Choices*, ©1983 Girls Incorporated of Greater Santa Barbara, Advocacy Press, Santa Barbara, CA.

What does this information tell you about gender bias in the workplace?

_____

_____

_____

_____

_____

What actions do you think you could take to make others aware of the bias?

_____

_____

_____

_____

_____

How can the bias be changed?

_____

_____

_____

_____

LESSON FIVE —Non-traditional Jobs and Careers

Career Scramble

Match the following occupations with a person from the list below. List only one individual.

Pilot   _____

Network News Anchor   _____

Astronaut   _____

Race Car Driver   _____

Congressperson   _____

Vice Presidential Candidate   _____

Union Leader   _____

Olympic Track Athlete   _____

Supreme Court Justice   _____

Surgeon General   _____

Attorney General   _____

Bank Robber   _____

Bess Coleman	Robert Kennedy
Robert Dole	Clarence Thomas
Mario Andretti	Norma Rae
Peter Jennings	Amelia Earhart
Ruth Bader Ginsberg	Neil Armstrong
C. Everett Koop	Bonnie Parker
Charles Lindbergh	Janet Reno
Sally Ride	Jocelyn Elders
Janet Guthrie	Connie Chung
Geraldine Ferraro	Jim Thorpe
Jesse James	Jackie Joyner Kersey
Patricia Schroeder	Caesar Chavez
Albert Gore	Edward Kennedy

This exercise is adapted from *Adolescent Parent Resource Guide,* Ohio Department of Education, p. 973, printed with permission.

LESSON SIX — Laws and Sexual Harassment

Each person is entitled to his or her personal space. Personal space is an imaginary boundary which each of us draws around our body. We are not comfortable when another individual crosses that boundary without our permission. When that space is violated we have the right to tell them to stop. If they will not stop, we have the right to report that person to some authority. The authority could be a parent, teacher, principal, supervisor at work, or law enforcement officer. Disrespecting a person's personal space can range from just poor manners to breaking the law. Sometimes it can be very confusing to define when that intrusion ceases to be inappropriate and becomes illegal.

Below write the definitions for the following:

Sexual Harassment _____

_____

_____

_____

Relationship Rights _____

_____

_____

_____

Cycle of Violence _____

_____

_____

_____

In the space below draw something that illustrates the *Cycle of Violence.*

List at least five types of behavior that have been identified by the *American Association of University Women* as behavior that could be a part of a pattern of harassment:

_____

_____

_____

_____

_____

Write about one example of sexual harassment that you think exists in our school and one action you think could be taken to decrease sexual harassment.

_____

_____

_____

_____

_____

_____

_____

_____

_____

_____

_____

_____

_____

_____

_____

_____

_____

The activity we are going to do today is called "Which Is It?" Take a few minutes to complete this activity and be able to support your answer.

Which Is It? *Violence, Sexual Harassment, Acceptable Behavior?*

Behavior:	Violence	Sexual Harassment	Acceptable Behavior	Not Sure
1. Boy grabs girl by the hair				
2. Man opens door for a woman				
3. Girl pinches boy's buttocks				
4. Girl offers to help boy baby-sit for younger sister				
5. Boy "whistles" at girl				
6. Boy snaps girl's bra				
7. Girl helps boy carry the balls and bats to the equipment room				
8. Woman invites male secretary to happy hour after work				
9. Boss tells "dirty jokes" at the office				
10. Female boss tells male employee he looks good in tight blue jeans				
11. Boy threatens to tell friends they've gone "all the way" if girlfriend doesn't give him answers to a math assignment				
12. Male boss tells female employee he likes the way her dress shows off her figure				
13. Boy slaps his date because he saw her flirting with someone else				
14. Girl hits her boyfriend because she heard he was with another girl				
15. Man hits his wife because she was talking to a male neighbor				
16. Woman bakes cake for single male employee's birthday				

LESSON SEVEN — Sex-Role Stereotyping

Complete the following sentence stems:

Girls are. . . (think of some names that boys call girls)

_____

_____

_____

Boys are. . . (think of some names that girls call boys)

_____

_____

_____

Girls can. . . (think of things that girls can do that boys can't do)

_____

_____

Boys can. . . (think of things that boys can do that girls can't do)

_____

_____

For Girls:

I like being a girl because. . . _____

_____

If I were a boy I could. . . _____

_____

For Boys:

I like being a boy because. . . _____

_____

If I were a girl I could. . . _____

_____

For Everyone:

Look at your responses

1. What do they tell you about the way you feel about sex roles?

_____

_____

2. How can sex-role stereotyping be limiting for females? For males?

_____

_____

3. What are some things you can do to neutralize or eliminate sex-role stereotyping in your own life?

_____

_____

LESSON EIGHT — Gender Exploitation in the Media

Listen to some of your favorite songs. Find one that has a message about gender. In the space below write that message.

_____

_____

_____

How does the message portray females?

_____

_____

How does the message portray males?

_____

_____

_____

During the next week, look for and write about at least one incident on TV or video or in music or print that portrays

1. Your gender in a positive way

_____

_____

2. Your gender in a negative way

_____

_____

3. The opposite gender in a positive way

_____

_____

_____

4. The opposite gender in a negative way

_____

_____

_____

5. Which was easier to find?

_____

_____

_____

LESSON NINE — Male and Female Roles in Parenting

Parenting Survey

As you read the following statements decide whether you *Agree, Disagree,* or are *Not Sure.*
Then place an X in the space that best describes what you think.

	Agree	Disagree	Not Sure
1. Having children is the only way a boy becomes a man.			
2. Couples shouldn't limit the number of children they have.			
3. Having children is a financial burden which causes stress.			
4. Children should always be loyal to their parents.			
5. Unless they have children, a couple is not accepted by their friends and relatives.			
6. Having children automatically makes people behave more responsibly.			
7. Parenting children causes arguments and stress between a husband and wife.			
8. Most women want to have children.			
9. Men have the responsibility for carrying on the family name by having children.			
10. Having children helps you feel more loved and less lonely.			
11. If a child gets into trouble, it is the parents' fault.			
12. Before a woman can be respected in our family, she must become a mother.			
13. A marriage isn't complete until a couple has children.			
14. Parents have the right to take the credit for the achievements of their children.			

	Agree	Disagree	Not Sure
15. The main reason people have children is because they have created something that will live on after they die.			
16. The family is the only group of people in which a person can feel happy and safe.			
17. Boring is the word to describe the job of staying home to take care of children.			
18. It is natural for men to want to have children.			
19. Before a couple has children they should think of the negative things that will happen to their relationship.			
20. A marriage becomes stronger when a couple has children.			
21. We all have a responsibility to have children some day.			
22. If a person doesn't have children, family traditions will die.			
23. Children should help take care of their parents when they grow old.			
24. Becoming a parent puts greater pressure on people to succeed in life.			
25. Having children is one of the most important purposes in life.			
26. Before becoming romantically involved with a man, a woman should think about whether he would make a good parent.			
27. It is ok to have a child with someone even though you quarrel a lot.			
28. It is important to know someone well before you marry and have children.			
29. Our parents should help us decide who we should marry.			
30. Sharing the same religious beliefs makes a family stronger.			
31. Relationships always improve after a couple gets married and has children.			

	Agree	Disagree	Not Sure
32. It's ok to marry someone you don't know very well because marriage will change both of you.			
33. Someone with younger brothers and/or sisters doesn't need to learn parenting skills.			
34. Being parents is the cause of most marriage problems.			
35. Being a good parent requires having a good sense of humor.			
36. Unhappy women should have children so they can feel loved.			
37. All of the work that goes into parenting never pays off.			
38. A woman should decide whether having children would interfere with her career.			
39. People without children are never as happy as those who have children.			
40. A couple with common interests would make good parents.			
41. Sharing household tasks is a sign of a healthy family.			
42. Having children around all of the time causes a lot of stress.			
43. Women who criticize their husbands a lot are still good mothers.			
44. A good reason to have children is so you can do a better job than your parents did with you.			
45. It's ok to have a child with someone who has told you he or she doesn't really want children.			

This exercise is adapted from *Adolescent Parent Resource Guide,* Ohio Department of Education, pp. 610-611.

Feelings/Action Worksheet

Today we are going to think about what it would be like to be the parent of a baby when it is crying. Use the space below to complete this exercise as your teacher gives you instructions.

FEELING   ACTION

1. _____   1. _____

                                     _____

                                     _____

                                     _____

2. _____   2. _____

                                     _____

                                     _____

                                     _____

3. _____   3. _____

                                     _____

                                     _____

                                     _____

Interview the parent of a young infant. If you do not know anyone who currently has an infant, interview a parent and ask them to try to remember when their child was a small infant and answer the questions accordingly.

1. Does your baby cry every day? _____ If so, approximately how much (just an average amount of time)?

2. When does your baby cry? _____
   (This answer might not be a specific time.)

3. What are the most common reasons your baby cries?

_____

_____

_____

_____

4. What are some of the actions you take when your baby cries?

_____

_____

_____

_____

5. How do you feel when the baby first cries?

_____

_____

When he/she continues to cry for an extended period of time?

_____

_____

_____

_____

LESSON TEN — Attitudes and Expectations About Parenting

In the space below complete the following sentence stems. The last one is optional because most of you probably would not choose to be a teen parent. If, however, you really believe that you do, complete the sentence and then evaluate your reasons. Are they sound? Parenting is a long-term responsibility that requires many skills. Do you think you will have the necessary skills if you should become a parent?

1. A parent is. . .

   _____

2. Being a parent means. . .

   _____

3. Being a teen parent would be. . .

   _____

4. I want to be a parent who. . .

   _____

5. I don't want to be a parent who. . .

   _____

6. I don't want to be a teen parent because. . .

   _____

7. I want to be a parent when. . .

   _____

   Optional: I *want* to be a teen parent because. . .

   _____

Skills and Qualities a Parent Must Possess

In the space below write a paragraph to complete one of the following statements:

I think parental responsibilities are the same for men and women and those responsibilities are. . . .

_____

_____

_____

_____

_____

_____

I think parental responsibilities are different for men and women and those responsibilities are. . . .

_____

_____

_____

_____

_____

_____

CHAPTER TWO — CULTURAL DIVERSITY

LESSON ONE — Valuing Self and Others

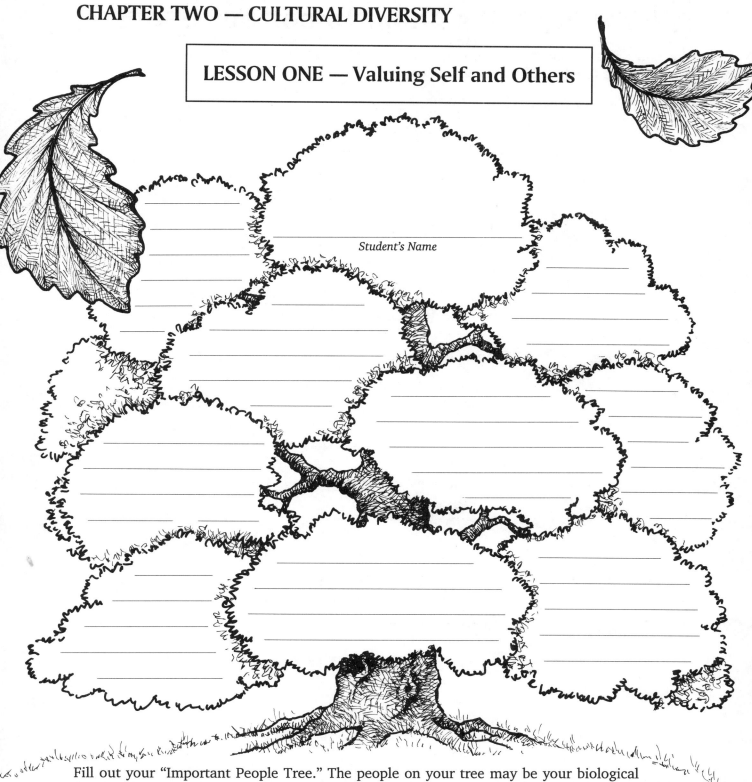

Student's Name

Fill out your "Important People Tree." The people on your tree may be your biological family (those people related to you by blood), important people in your life, or a combination of family members and others who influence your life.

Please note that not only are you asked to write the people's names, but beneath their names you are asked to put the quality that makes them important.

The Family Talks About Important Issues

Directions: The student and appropriate family members are invited to discuss the following topics and the family's values on each.

1. Male/female roles: Family response: _____

    _____

    _____

    _____

    Student response: _____

    _____

    _____

    _____

2. Drug use: Family response: _____

    _____

    _____

    _____

    Student response: _____

    _____

    _____

    _____

3. Teenage parents: Family response: _____

    _____

    _____

    _____

    Student response: _____

    _____

    _____

    _____

4. Gender bias: Family response: _____

_____

_____

_____

Student response: _____

_____

_____

_____

5. Fathers as   Family response: _____
   homemakers:

_____

_____

_____

Student response: _____

_____

_____

_____

6. Friendship: Family response: _____

_____

_____

_____

Student response: _____

_____

_____

_____

7. Divorce: Family response: _____

_____

_____

_____

Student response: _____

_____

_____

_____

8. Birth control: Family response: _____

_____

_____

_____

Student response: _____

_____

_____

_____

9. Showing   Family response: _____
    affection:
_____

_____

_____

Student response: _____

_____

_____

_____

10. Having
    children:

Family response: _____

_____

_____

_____

Student response: _____

_____

_____

_____

11. Premarital
    sex:

Family response: _____

_____

_____

_____

Student response: _____

_____

_____

_____

12. Education

Family response: _____

_____

_____

_____

Student response: _____

_____

_____

_____

13. Marriage: Family response: _____

                           _____

                           _____

                           _____

                           Student response: _____

                           _____

                           _____

                           _____

14. Love: Family response: _____

                           _____

                           _____

                           _____

                           Student response: _____

                           _____

                           _____

                           _____

15. Spirituality or   Family response: _____
    religion:
                           _____

                           _____

                           _____

                           Student response: _____

                           _____

                           _____

                           _____

16. Creativity: Family response: _____

_____

_____

_____

Student response: _____

_____

_____

_____

17. Other

_____: Family response: _____

_____

_____

_____

Student response: _____

_____

_____

_____

18. Other

_____: Family response: _____

_____

_____

_____

Student response: _____

_____

_____

_____

19. Other   Family response: _____

    _____ :   _____

                            _____

                            _____

                            Student response: _____

                            _____

                            _____

                            _____

20. Other   Family response: _____

    _____ :   _____

                            _____

                            _____

                            Student response: _____

                            _____

                            _____

                            _____

As you move toward greater independence, it is important to examine your own values.

Are they the same as your family's? Are they different? Which of your values are the most important to you? How are they influenced by how your family feels?

Write your answers to these questions in **Thoughts for Today**.

LESSON TWO — Appreciating Differences

Each individual in our society is unique and special. Including all members of society as equal has many benefits but many times it is difficult to achieve diversity in our communities because there are many barriers. In the spaces below write your thoughts about the benefits of diversity and the barriers to achieving diversity.

MY THOUGHTS:

1. I think the benefits of diversity are. . . .

_____

_____

_____

2. I think the barriers to achieving diversity are. . . .

_____

_____

_____

Interview someone that you listed on your "Important People Tree." Below list his/her thoughts about the benefits of and barriers to achieving diversity.

_____'S THOUGHTS:

Name of person who completes this page with you

1. I think the benefits of diversity are. . . .

_____

_____

_____

2. I think the barriers to achieving diversity are. . . .

_____

_____

_____

LESSON THREE — Strengthening Group Cohesion

Read the information below.

Many times we feel that we can do something better by ourselves than if we have to work as part of a group. We certainly do need to learn to be self-sufficient, to learn to be self-reliant and make decisions for ourselves, but many times being a part of a group and working together for a common goal has great benefits.

Think of our forefathers as they settled the West. The pioneers were much more likely to reach their destination when they traveled in a group across the country. By banding their wagons together in a wagon train, they could share their expertise and resources as they made the difficult trip across the country. One person might know how to "shoe" the horses, another how to cook and another how to interpret the geography on a map with few features. Someone else might have been a good trapper or hunter.

By pooling their talents and resources they were all much more likely to reach their destination.

Today we participated in an activity called, "The whole is greater than the sum of its parts."

In the space below summarize what you learned from this activity:

_____

_____

_____

_____

In the space below answer the following question: Would you usually like to work as part of a team or alone and why?

_____

_____

_____

_____

LESSON FOUR — Cultural Stereotypes

There are many groups that we stereotype. List at least five different groupings.
An example would be A RELIGIOUS GROUP.

List at least one way we stereotype in our society and the impact you think that has:

_____

_____

_____

_____

Complete the following sentence: I think one type of stereotyping that exists
in our school is. . . .

_____

_____

_____

_____

and one concrete thing we could do to help eliminate it would be. . .

_____

_____

_____

_____

_____

LESSON FIVE — The Price of Prejudice

Differences are not necessarily bad or good; they are just different.

One important thing for us to remember is that each one of us is a unique human being. There isn't a single person who is exactly like another human being. Even identical twins who look exactly alike have different thoughts, ideas, and talents. It is important to remember that our prejudices can be limiting and harmful. Celebrating our differences can make us a better class, school, community, country and world.

In the space below complete the following sentences:

Being different means. . . .

_____

_____

I felt different when. . . .

_____

_____

Complete the following questions:

1. Why do we sometimes see differences as positive at one time and negative at another?

   _____

2. If we have strong negative feelings about someone who is different, what can happen?

   _____

3. What do you do when you feel uncomfortable with someone who is different?

   _____

4. Do you act differently toward them?

   _____

5. How can seeing differences as negative lead to prejudging someone (prejudice)?

   _____

LESSON SIX — Designing Our Own Community

Imagine that you have a magic wand and you can design the "Ideal School, Community, Country or World." Decide which you would design and write a paragraph below describing your ideal place.

BOOK TWO

Personal Development

CHAPTER THREE — ADOLESCENT DEVELOPMENT

LESSON ONE — Physical and Emotional Changes

List below the things you like *best* about being an adolescent.

_____

_____

_____

_____

List below the three things you like *least* about being an adolescent.

_____

_____

_____

_____

If you were the parent of an adolescent, what would be the most important thing you could give to your child?

_____

_____

_____

_____

There are many things about adolescent development that you cannot change but there are some things you can do to make the this stage of life more comfortable for you. What are some of those things?

_____

_____

_____

_____

LESSON TWO — Social Development

Whenever we do something to help someone else, it enhances our own self esteem. Helping others is a positive way to reinforce good feelings in ourselves. It is important to be good to ourselves, too! Fill in the spaces below to record things you can do for others and for yourself.

Write down one thing you could do to make *another person* feel good.

_____

_____

_____

_____

Think about something you could do to make *yourself* feel good. **Be sure you remember to do it!**

_____

_____

_____

_____

Write down one thing you wish *all people* would do to make them feel good about themselves.

_____

_____

_____

_____

LESSON THREE — Intellectual Development

Read the Case Studies below. Identify the problem. Help the individual with the problem develop a plan to deal with the problem.

Nancy was invited to go bowling with her friends. She said she didn't want to go because she didn't know how to bowl. After a lot of coaxing, she gave in and went along with the group to the bowling alley. On the way, she was trying to think of another excuse so she wouldn't have to bowl. She was really afraid that she would do something stupid and her friends would laugh at her. After she arrived, she let her friends order shoes and pick out a ball for her. The bowling alley was full of people. When it came her turn, Nancy got up to bowl and dropped the ball behind her on the first try. Feeling humiliated, she ran crying to the restroom.

The family was planning to go to Uncle Ed's for the weekend. Mom and Dad had planned the outing several weeks ago. Sammy was expected to go along so he could baby-sit for his younger brother and sister while Mom and Dad and Uncle Ed went to the ball game. Sammy wanted to stay home and go skating with his friends. Sammy told his parents he had asked his best friend if he could spend the weekend with him. Mom and Dad refused his request,

Juanita and her mother, Carlotta, went shopping for school clothes. Juanita knew exactly what she wanted to buy, but her mother insisted on going along. "After all," she said, "it's my money we are spending and I want to make sure it is spent wisely." Carlotta thought Juanita looked good in red, but Juanita was tired of that color. She wanted to buy a black blouse with see-through lace on the sleeves. Carlotta refused to buy it saying, "I don't care if the other girls *are* wearing clothes like this, this blouse makes you look too old!"

Juan invited Barbie to the school dance. Barbie's dad wasn't happy that she accepted because he didn't know Juan's family. He wasn't happy that she was dating in the first place, but this made him even more unhappy! When Juan came to pick up Barbie, he stopped in front of the house and honked the horn for her to come out. Barbie's dad went out and said, "If you can't come to the door like a gentleman, my daughter can't go with you—get lost!"

Expectations

You expect things *for* yourself and *from* yourself. Others have expectations of you, too. Think about what your parents and the community expect from you in *different roles*. Complete the chart below. Some of these spaces may be difficult for you to complete. If you don't know the answers, this would be a good time to talk with your parents or a caring adult to help you complete them.

WHAT DO YOUR PARENTS AND THE COMMUNITY EXPECT FROM YOU SOCIALLY AND EMOTIONALLY IN THE FOLLOWING ROLES?

Role	Social/Emotional	How Does This Expectation Feel?
Student		
Daughter/Son		
Friend		
Self		
Other		

Answer the following questions:

a. Are there similarities and/or differences in the expectations you have for yourself and others have for you?

_____

_____

b. Where there are differences, does this now cause or do you anticipate that it will cause conflicts or problems?

_____

_____

CHAPTER FOUR — SELF ESTEEM

LESSON ONE — Self Assessment

How Well Do You Like Yourself?

Complete the survey below, using the following scores:

15 if it's true almost all of the time
10 if it's true most of the time
5 if it's sometimes true
0 if it's seldom true

_____ 1. I am kind and loving.

_____ 2. I am an optimistic person.

_____ 3. I make friends easily.

_____ 4. I am happy with my life the way it is.

_____ 5. I look forward to each new day.

_____ 6. I would rather be me than anyone else.

_____ 7. If I were someone else, I would choose me for my friend.

_____ 8. When I feel strongly about something, it feels good to express my feelings.

_____ 9. Regardless of my grades, I feel good about the work I do.

_____ 10. Other people treat me nicely most of the time.

_____ 11. My life is very interesting.

_____ 12. Most of the time I am in a good mood.

_____ 13. When I make a mistake I can laugh at myself.

_____ 14. My energy level is usually high.

_____ 15. I get plenty of exercise and eat well.

_____ 16. I am happy with the way I look.

_____ 17. If I were a person of the opposite sex, I would want to ask me for a date.

_____ 18. My friends and family value my ideas and listen to what I say.

Scale For Self Esteem

200-225	Very high self esteem, positive self-worth. You like yourself.
120-195	Self-esteem and self worth are good. You accept yourself and your life. Self image could be improved with conscious effort.
45 -115	Self esteem is so-so. Acceptance of yourself and your self worth is less than desirable. You need to work on improving your self image. You may want to practice being your own best friend and follow some of the advice given below.
Below 45	Very low self esteem and self worth. Health and personal growth could suffer. You need to develop relationships which give you encouragement and support. You also need to work on changing your own negative attitudes and behaviors. It might help to talk about this with someone you trust. Try to practice the advice given below.

One of the best ways to improve our self esteem is to be nice to ourselves. Begin saying nice things to yourself. Start each day with a positive comment to yourself about yourself and reinforce that comment throughout the day.

Surround yourself with positive people and people who are positive about you. Don't allow others to put you down.

Accept yourself as you are right now and begin to work to change those things that you don't like or want to improve about yourself.

Set goals for yourself — small, medium and large. Congratulate yourself as you accomplish even the smallest of goals.

Substitute "I can" and "I'll do my best" for "I can't" in your vocabulary. Begin to see yourself as successful and capable of reaching your goals.

START NOW AND NEVER GIVE UP!

This exercise is adapted from *Adolescent Parent Resource Guide,* Ohio Department of Education, p. 73.

Personal Ship

Complete your Personal Ship by writing or drawing something in the numbered space which corresponds with the numbers below and would indicate the answers to the following questions:

1. My favorite possession
2. What I do best
3. Greatest success in the past 12 months
4. Unrestrained by money and commitments, what I would do in the next 12 months
5. Three words that best describe me
6. What I am really trying to get better at
7. Three successful experiences I've had in my life (fun and success)
8. Biggest mistake that I learned from
9. Three words I would like people to use to describe me

LESSON TWO — Positive Approach to Personal Empowerment

Write five CONCRETE things you can do to enhance your self esteem.

Here's an example which you may use if you'd like: I will take responsibility for my own life; my successes and my failures.

1. _____

2. _____

3. _____

4. _____

5. _____

Now write one specific action you will take to improve your self esteem today! This example should be very concrete.

_____
_____
_____
_____
_____
_____
_____

Now write one specific action you will take to enhance someone else's self esteem. This can be a friend or family member.

_____
_____
_____
_____
_____
_____

LESSON THREE — Self Talk

On the SHORT LINES below write your first and last name vertically, putting one letter on each line. On the longer line next to each letter, write a positive adjective that begins with that letter. For example, Mary: **M - marvelous**, **A – able**, **R – reliable**, **Y – youthful**.

First Name   Last Name

_____ _____   _____ _____

_____ _____   _____ _____

_____ _____   _____ _____

_____ _____   _____ _____

_____ _____   _____ _____

_____ _____   _____ _____

_____ _____   _____ _____

_____ _____   _____ _____

_____ _____   _____ _____

_____ _____   _____ _____

_____ _____   _____ _____

_____ _____   _____ _____

_____ _____   _____ _____

_____ _____   _____ _____

_____ _____   _____ _____

Myself and Others Chart

	My Opinion of Me	Others' Opinion of Me
My Intelligence		
My Appearance		
My Goals		
My Talents		
My Personality		
My Responsibility		
I As a Friend		
I As a Parent (Now)		
I As a Parent (In the future)		

1. Are your opinions of yourself higher or lower than the opinions you perceive others have of you? Why or why not?

_____

_____

2. How do you feel about the similarities and/or differences?

_____

_____

In the space below write a positive self-talk phrase that you will begin to say to yourself each morning when you awaken. Record this phrase in your **Thoughts for Today** as well as here.

_____

_____

_____

This exercise is adapted from *Adolescent Parent Resouce Guide,* Ohio Department of Education p. 78, printed with permission.

LESSON FOUR — Taking Charge

The following are definitions for **Assertive**, **Aggressive** and **Passive** behaviors:

Assertive: Standing up for yourself; acting in your own best interest but doing so with regard for others' feelings. Stating your thoughts, desires or feelings with

- ◆ clear, direct statements
- ◆ direct eye contact
- ◆ respect, showing concern for others' feelings

Aggressive: Saying what you think or doing what you want regardless of anyone else's feelings.

- ◆ pushing your views on others
- ◆ showing no respect for others' feelings or rights

Passive: Taking no action in order to avoid conflict. You have feelings and desires but you do not express them openly.

While being respectful of other people's rights, YOU HAVE THE RIGHT TO:

- ◆ Ask for what you want
- ◆ Refuse someone else's request
- ◆ Change your mind if you make a decision that isn't in your best interest.

Complete the following sentence: I think acting assertively is the best choice because

_____

_____

_____

_____

Write about a situation that has either happened to you or you see happening in your school or community. Think about how you could act assertively to be helpful. Refer to the definitions above to help you understand the term *assertive*. Put this on a separate piece of paper so you can turn it in to the teacher; however, you may also want to jot it down in the space below so that you can remember the situation you selected.

_____

_____

_____

_____

CHAPTER FIVE — CREATING YOUR DREAM

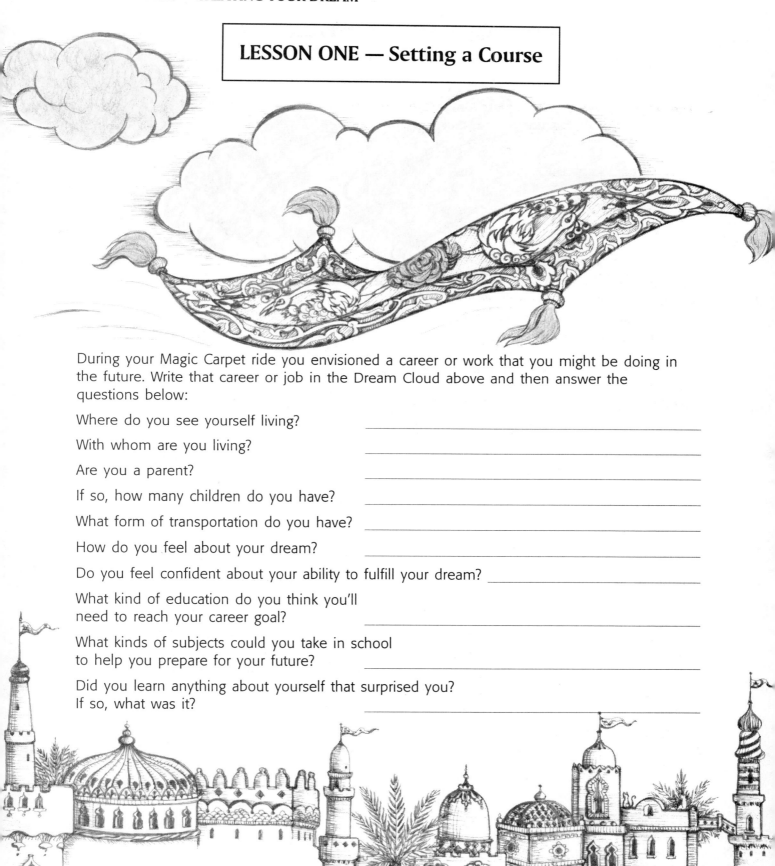

LESSON ONE — Setting a Course

During your Magic Carpet ride you envisioned a career or work that you might be doing in the future. Write that career or job in the Dream Cloud above and then answer the questions below:

Where do you see yourself living? _____

With whom are you living? _____

Are you a parent? _____

If so, how many children do you have? _____

What form of transportation do you have? _____

How do you feel about your dream? _____

Do you feel confident about your ability to fulfill your dream? _____

What kind of education do you think you'll
need to reach your career goal? _____

What kinds of subjects could you take in school
to help you prepare for your future? _____

Did you learn anything about yourself that surprised you?
If so, what was it? _____

LESSON TWO — Setting and Attaining Goals

Think of a time you've tried something new and accomplished or completed the task. In the space below write down what that was and how you felt.

_____

_____

_____

In *Chapter One—Lesson One*, we talked about the **Explorer With A Plan**. Think about the Explorer you chose. As you think about that explorer, answer the questions below. Some of the questions may require some guessing on your part, but that's OK because we might not be absolutely sure of the answers.

List three short-term or small goals that the explorer had. After each goal, list how you think that person felt when she/he accomplished that goal.

1. _____

Feeling: _____

2. _____

Feeling: _____

3. _____

Feeling: _____

Do the same for long-range goals.

1. _____

Feeling: _____

2. _____

Feeling: _____

3. _____

Feeling: _____

Below list three short-term goals (things you want to accomplish by the end of the week). Beside each goal write one to three action steps that you will take to accomplish this goal.

When you complete these goals, come back to this page and write how you felt when this goal was accomplished.

Goal #1. _____

Action Steps: _____

_____

_____

_____

Feeling: _____

Goal #2. _____

Action Steps: _____

_____

_____

_____

Feeling: _____

Goal #3. _____

Action Steps: _____

_____

_____

_____

Feeling: _____

Now list three medium-range goals (things that can be accomplished within the next month). Beside each goal write one to three action steps that you will take to accomplish this goal.

When you complete these goals, come back to this page and write how you felt when this goal was accomplished.

Goal #1. _____

Action Steps: _____

_____

_____

_____

Feeling: _____

Goal #2. _____

Action Steps: _____

_____

_____

_____

Feeling: _____

Goal #3. _____

Action Steps: _____

_____

_____

_____

Feeling: _____

And finally list three long-range goals (things you can accomplish within the next year or two). Beside each goal write one to three action steps that you will take to accomplish this goal.

When you complete these goals, come back to this page and write how you felt when this goal was accomplished.

Goal #1. _____

Action Steps: _____

_____

_____

_____

Feeling: _____

Goal #2. _____

Action Steps: _____

_____

_____

_____

Feeling: _____

Goal #3. _____

Action Steps: _____

_____

_____

_____

Feeling: _____

LESSON THREE — Personal Planning

Refer back to your "Dream Cloud" on page 67 of your workbook and list the career or occupation you want to plan for. Remember this may change many times as you learn and grow. You can do a plan for many careers as you change your mind.

Complete the career plan below. The first short-term goal is completed for you as an example. You complete the action steps and additional goals.

My Career Goal: _____

Short-Term Goals: Action Steps:

1. Learn as much as possible about   1. _____
   this career.   2. _____
                                            3. _____
                                            4. _____
                                            5. _____

2. _____   1. _____
   _____   2. _____
                                            3. _____
                                            4. _____
                                            5. _____

3. _____   1. _____
   _____   2. _____
                                            3. _____
                                            4. _____
                                            5. _____

Medium-Range Goals:

1. _____   1. _____
   _____   2. _____
                                            3. _____
                                            4. _____
                                            5. _____

2. _____   1. _____
   _____   2. _____
                                            3. _____
                                            4. _____
                                            5. _____

Long-Range Goal: Action Steps:

1. _____   1. _____
   _____   2. _____
                                          3. _____
                                          4. _____
                                          5. _____

Next look at your first short-term goal. Let's break it down into a real *work plan*.

Goal: Learn as much as possible about

Action Steps   By When: Resources needed and/or who can help:

1. _____   _____   _____
                                                _____
                                                _____
                                                _____

2. _____   _____   _____
                                                _____
                                                _____
                                                _____

3. _____   _____   _____
                                                _____
                                                _____
                                                _____

4. _____   _____   _____
                                                _____
                                                _____
                                                _____

5. _____   _____   _____
                                                _____
                                                _____
                                                _____

Use a form such as this to plan how you will achieve your goals. Perhaps you can't fill in all the spaces now but a work plan is something that is just that—a plan! You can add to it and you can change it. The page which follows is a blank work plan sheet. Copy it as many times as you need to to complete all your goals in the form of a work plan.

Work Plan

Name: _____

Goal: _____

_____

Action Steps   By When: Resources needed and/or who can help:

1. _____   _____   _____
   _____   _____
   _____   _____
   _____   _____

2. _____   _____   _____
   _____   _____
   _____   _____
   _____   _____

3. _____   _____   _____
   _____   _____
   _____   _____
   _____   _____

4. _____   _____   _____
   _____   _____
   _____   _____
   _____   _____

5. _____   _____   _____
   _____   _____
   _____   _____
   _____   _____

LESSON FOUR — Mastering Skills

1. In the space below make a list of things you have to do and attitudes you have to have to be able to "master a new skill."

   _____

   _____

2. Respond to the following statements:
   a. "The more you practice a new skill, the easier it becomes."

   _____

   b. "Fear of failure can prevent an individual from reaching his/her potential."

   _____

3. Write the name of at least one skill that you currently possess that you think is your most important skill and write a sentence or two to explain why this skill is so important.

   _____

   _____

Turn to page 209 and record this skill in your "Skill Box."

4. List at least three skills which you will need to master in order to graduate from high school.

   _____

   _____

5. List at least three skills which you don't possess today which you would need before you become a parent.

   _____

   _____

CHAPTER SIX — SKILL DEVELOPMENT

LESSON ONE — Communication

Read the following situations below and change the "you messages" to "I messages" using the example below to help guide you.

1. *State the feeling or problem*
   I feel very angry. . .

2. *Describe the behavior*
   . . . when I find dirty dishes all over the kitchen.

3. *Because*
   I don't think it is fair to the rest of the family.

4. *Explain what you want*
   I want you to go to the kitchen and do the dishes.

The key is to remember the following points:
- ◆ Feeling
- ◆ Behavior
- ◆ Why
- ◆ What

Name the feeling you are having, name the behavior that causes that feeling, state why that is so, and what you want to have happen.

You are a parent and your child is always leaving her toys all over the floor. You have spoken to her over and over. Finally one afternoon, you blow up and say, "You are such a bad child! You never do anything I tell you to do. You are making my life miserable!"

Instead you say:

State the feeling: *I feel* _____

Name the behavior: *when* _____

Why: *because* _____

What: *I want* _____

Your boyfriend/girlfriend is always late. It really annoys you and you have told him/her so over and over. One day he/she is an hour late and you are really angry. You want to say, "You inconsiderate creep! You make me so mad! You never think about anyone but yourself!"

Instead you say:

State the feeling: *I feel* _____

Name the behavior: *when* _____

Why: *because* _____

What: *I want* _____

Below write a situation that is relevant to you or someone you know (do not use real names because you will be sharing this situation with a classmate).

_____

_____

_____

_____

_____

_____

_____

_____

_____

_____

_____

_____

Write the response (I message) that was given when you shared your situation.

State the feeling: *I feel* _____

Name the behavior: *when* _____

Why: *because* _____

What: *I want* _____

LESSON TWO — Active Listening

Complete the following:

Write *barriers* to effective communication.

_____

_____

_____

_____

Write *guidelines* to effective communication.

_____

_____

_____

_____

Record *feeling* words.

_____

_____

_____

_____

My communication strengths are. . . .

_____   My communication weaknesses are. . . .

_____   _____

_____   _____

_____   _____

_____   _____

                                           _____

                                           _____

Look at the items you listed under weaknesses. List at least one concrete action you will take to improve your communication skills.

_____

_____

LESSON THREE — Decision Making

Record a decision-making model below: This should be the same model you used in *Chapter Four, Lesson Four*.

_____

_____

_____

_____

_____

_____

_____

_____

_____

_____

_____

_____

_____

_____

Write a situation in which you can use the decision-making model above. You will later develop a role play about this situation or a situation that one of your classmates suggests.

_____

_____

_____

_____

_____

_____

_____

_____

_____

_____

LESSON FOUR — Refusal Skills

Write about a typical situation in which a person might need to refuse a request or change his/her mind.

_____

_____

_____

_____

Script a role play in which the main character refuses a request or changes his/her mind. Be sure you use good communication and assertiveness techniques.

_____

_____

_____

_____

_____

_____

_____

_____

_____

_____

_____

_____

_____

_____

_____

_____

LESSON FIVE — Managing Time

Divide the circles below into "typical" days as labeled. Each circle is divided into eight equal sections so each section equals three hours. If you have activities that take less than three hours, subdivide some sections.

My Current Day

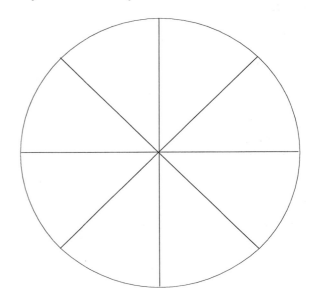

If I Were A Teenage Parent

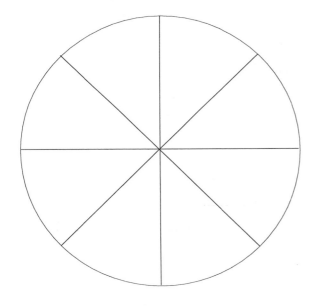

My Ideal Day

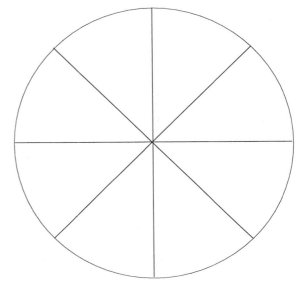

Use your "Ideal Day" as a guide to help you plan your week. Fill in the first page with what you think you will be doing during the next week. Use the second page to record exactly what does occur.

Sample Weekly Planner

Sunday

_____

_____

Monday

_____

_____

Tuesday

_____

_____

Wednesday

_____

_____

Thursday

_____

_____

Friday

_____

_____

Saturday

_____

_____

Actual Week's Events:

Sunday
_____
_____

Monday
_____
_____

Tuesday
_____
_____

Wednesday
_____
_____

Thursday
_____
_____

Friday
_____
_____

Saturday
_____
_____
_____

LESSON SIX — Managing Your Mind

My Study Habits Self Assessment: Subjects, Grades, and Environment

Knowing how you feel about the subjects you are taking can help you design your study plan. Some students will want to tackle their "worst subjects" first and get them out of the way; others will want to tackle those subjects in small doses sandwiched in between subjects they like and enjoy. Completing the information below will help you focus on your likes and dislikes in school. Later you can use this information as you develop your study plan.

COMPLETE THE FOLLOWING:

The subjects I earn the best grades in are _____

_____

The subjects I earn the worst grades in are _____

_____

The subjects I like the best are _____

_____

The subjects I like the least are _____

_____

◆ Are the subjects you earn the best grades in, the ones you like the most or the least? _____ Why do you think this is true?

_____

_____

_____

◆ How can this information help you design your study plan? (Refer back to this answer when you develop your study plan.)

_____

_____

_____

Complete the assessment below. *There are no right or wrong answers.* This is a tool to help you focus on the best study plan for you.

THE BEST LEARNING AND STUDY ENVIRONMENT FOR ME IS . . . .

1. I enjoy learning most when
   _____ listening to a lecture
   _____ watching a demonstration
   _____ participating in an activity or demonstration
   _____ doing all of the above

2. I consider myself to be a
   _____ visual learner (see)
   _____ oral/auditory learner (speak/listen)

3. In class I like to sit
   _____ in the front
   _____ in the back
   _____ near the door
   _____ near the window

Assess why you answered the above question the way you did. Does the place you prefer to sit enhance your learning skills or detract from your learning skills?

4. In order to help me concentrate in class I should sit
   _____ in the front
   _____ in the back
   _____ near the door
   _____ near the window

5. I prefer to study
   _____ in the morning before school
   _____ in the afternoon
   _____ in the evening
   _____ on the weekends in larger blocks of time
   _____ every day for a shorter period of time

6. I study best
   _____ when I am alone
   _____ with a friend
   _____ in a study group

7. I seem to learn the most if I
   _____ study one subject for a long period of time until I get it
   _____ study several subjects for shorter periods of time alternating those subjects

8. The place I study the best is
   _____ at a library
   _____ in my room
   _____ in front of the TV
   _____ at school where I can ask for help if needed

9. I accomplish more when studying if I take a break
   _____ at least every half hour
   _____ at least once an hour
   _____ every two hours

ASSIGNMENTS FOR THIS WEEK:

NUMBER *ONE* PRIORITY: _____

SUBJECT: _____

ASSIGNMENT: _____

_____

_____

_____

DAY & TIME TO BE DONE: _____

PLACE TO BE DONE: _____

WITH WHOM: _____

NUMBER *TWO* PRIORITY: _____

SUBJECT: _____

ASSIGNMENT: _____

_____

_____

_____

DAY & TIME TO BE DONE: _____

PLACE TO BE DONE: _____

WITH WHOM: _____

NUMBER *THREE* PRIORITY: _____

SUBJECT: _____

ASSIGNMENT: _____

_____

_____

_____

DAY & TIME TO BE DONE: _____

PLACE TO BE DONE: _____

WITH WHOM: _____

LESSON SEVEN — Knowing When You Succeed

Remember the "Dream Cloud" that you did several lessons ago?

We are going to do some more visioning. This time we are going to think about success. Develop a vision of success for yourself and write it in the space below.

Success for me would mean. . . .

_____

_____

_____

The following would contribute to my success. . . .

_____

_____

_____

Perhaps during your life you have had a failure and that failure actually helped you succeed at a later time. Complete the following statement:

One way "failure" helped me succeed was. . . .

_____

_____

_____

LESSON EIGHT — Choosing Your Guides

Our role models are the individuals we pattern our own lives after.

Name your role model(s):

_____

Why do you think of them as role models for you?

_____

_____

_____

_____

What are the three most important qualities you look for in a friend and/or a role model?

_____

_____

_____

_____

Look back to *Chapter Two, Lesson One,* page 41 of your workbook. There you will find your "Important People Tree." What are the qualities listed most often on your tree?

_____

_____

Compare those qualities with the ones you listed for your role model(s) and your friends. Are they similar or different? Why do you think this is so?

_____

_____

_____

_____

Conflict Resolution

1. *Conflict* is defined as a situation where two opposing forces or individuals have different viewpoints, ideas, interests, needs, or internal or external demands which result in a struggle. Resolution comes from the word resolve. *Conflict resolution, therefore, is working together to resolve a conflict.* When two or more people work together to resolve a conflict, they need several skills. Below list some of the skills a person might need to resolve conflicts.

_____   _____

_____   _____

_____   _____

_____   _____

_____   _____

_____   _____

_____   _____

Many times the action that precipitates a conflict is the last of many actions which have occurred previously: *"The straw that broke the camel's back" syndrome!*

In order to help you understand what this means, read the example below.

2. Harry came home from school one day and threw his things down in the front hallway, where he knew they didn't belong. His mom saw them and exploded! He'd left them there everyday for the last week. Then, all she did was tell him to put them away. Why might she have blown up today?

_____

_____

_____

_____

Do you think this mom would have had this same reaction if this had only happened once? Probably not. Today was **"the straw that broke the camel's back!"** It happened one time too many.

3. How could this incident escalate into a conflict? Script the next events
   you think could lead to a major conflict between Harry and his mother.

_____

_____

_____

_____

Let's pretend that Harry and his mom have had a big fight as a result of the example we originally listed. It resulted in a major conflict for the reasons you listed. Harry was grounded. He was mad and thought it was unfair. His mother was mad and thought Harry was inconsiderate. Can Harry and his mom resolve this conflict?

Before Harry and his mom can resolve this conflict, both individuals need to understand what the problem is. Sometimes the problem is more than it appears on the surface. So the first step in **Conflict Resolution** is:

DEFINE THE PROBLEM

Using "I Messages" (refer back to *Lesson One* of this chapter) define the problem as seen by Harry's mom.

    I feel   _____

    when   _____

    because   _____

    I want   _____

Using "I Messages" define the problem as seen by Harry.

    I feel   _____

    when   _____

    because   _____

    I want   _____

Harry and his mom might resolve their problem if they used **REFLECTIVE LISTENING**. If they did, what feelings would be heard?

From Harry: From Harry's mom:

_____   _____

_____   _____

_____   _____

_____   _____

_____   _____

Generate a **LIST** of **SOLUTIONS** that might be acceptable to Harry and his mom. As you make this list remember that all solutions do not have to be acceptable to both. After a long list is generated, then Harry and his mom will use **NEGOTIATION SKILLS** to compromise to find one solution that is acceptable to both individuals.

_____   _____

_____   _____

_____   _____

_____   _____

_____   _____

_____   _____

Cross out any solution that you think **WOULD NOT** be acceptable to both Harry and his mom. Do you have one or more solutions left? If not, you will have to use patience and perseverance as you think of more solutions and work to find a compromise. Remember that _compromise_ means that each party may have to make concessions. When you have completed this process one or more times to **FIND AN ACCEPTABLE SOLUTION**, write your solution in the space below.

_____

_____

_____

_____

Once the solution has been identified, imagine how Harry and his mom would **IMPLEMENT THE SOLUTION** and **EVALUATE** how that implementation might work.

Don't forget the three "Ps" — Patience, Perseverance, and Practice!

The steps to **Conflict Resolution** are:

DEFINE THE PROBLEM
- ◆ **Use "I Messages"**
- ◆ **Practice "Reflective Listening"**

LIST SOLUTIONS
USE NEGOTIATION SKILLS
- ◆ **Select a Solution**
- ◆ **Implement the Solution**
- ◆ **Evaluate the Results**

Think of a recent conflict you have had. How did you resolve it? Did you use effective conflict resolution? If so, what were the results? If not, using the steps of conflict resolution, think about what might have happened if you did use this skill.

In your **Thoughts for Today** write what happened when you used conflict resolution. If you did not use conflict resolution, write what you think the result would have been if you did use this skill.

DON'T FORGET TO PUT YOUR NEW SKILLS IN THE SKILL BOX!

LESSON NINE — Managing Adversity

Complete the following:

List the three most important skills you think a teenager needs to have to cope with adversity.

_____

_____

_____

_____

_____

_____

In addition to those listed above, list three skills you think a teenage parent needs to have to cope with adversity.

_____

_____

_____

_____

_____

_____

Dress the stick figure in the skills a teenager needs to deal with adversity.

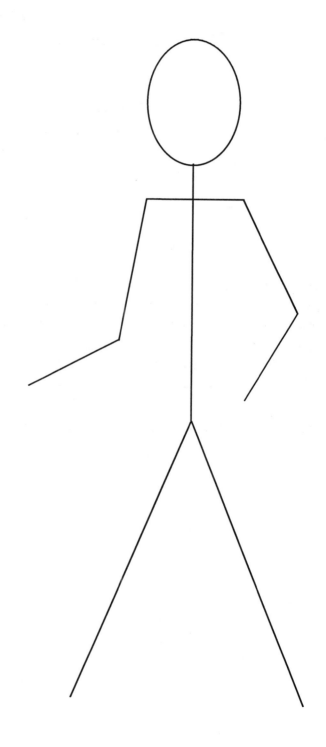

LESSON TEN — Commitments

Below list some of the types of commitments and/or contracts that a teenager might have. These may or may not pertain to you personally.

Commitments to self:

_____

_____

_____

_____

_____

Commitments to/with others:

_____

_____

_____

_____

_____

Select one commitment from each list and in the space below, write a short paragraph to explain what that commitment would require of the teenager. What skills would the teenager use in meeting the commitment?

Self: _____

_____

_____

_____

Others: _____

_____

_____

_____

Think of a personal commitment you would like to make to yourself.
Write the commitment below.

The commitment I would like to make to myself is _____

_____

_____

In order to make this commitment seem more concrete, use the space below to develop a contract with yourself. Have it witnessed by a classmate, teacher or family member.

Name: _____

Address: _____

Date of Contract: _____

Intent or purpose of contract:

I, _____, hereby make a commitment to

_____

_____

_____

_____

In order to accomplish the above, I
_____, will take the following action
(include the date if applicable):

_____ by _____(date).

_____ by _____(date).

_____ by _____(date).

Signed: _____ Date: _____

Witnessed by: _____ Date _____

Commitments a teenage parent might make that would be different from those of an adolescent who is not a parent:

To Self:

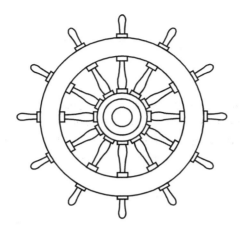

_____

_____

_____

_____

_____

_____

_____

_____

_____

_____

_____

To Partner:

_____

_____

_____

_____

_____

_____

_____

_____

_____

_____

To Child:

_____

_____

_____

_____

_____

_____

_____

_____

_____

_____

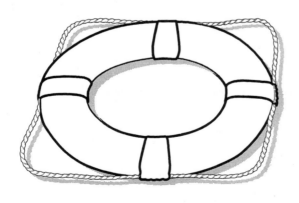

Think of a commitment you would like to make to someone else. This may be a friend, a teacher, or a family member. Talk with that person to learn a commitment they are willing to make to you. Write the commitment you both agree on below:

The commitment we would like to make to each other is _____

_____

_____

In order to make this commitment seem more concrete, use the space below to develop a contract between the parties involved. Have it witnessed by someone other than the parties involved in the commitment. Each person should have a copy of the contract.

Name: _____

Address: _____

Name: _____

Address: _____ Date of Contract: _____

Intent or purpose of contract:

I, _____, and I, _____, hereby

make a commitment to _____

_____

In order to accomplish the above, I _____,

will take the following action (include the date if applicable):

_____ by (date) _____

_____ by (date) _____

_____ by (date) _____

In order to accomplish the above, I _____, will take the following action (include the date if applicable):

_____ by (date) _____

_____ by (date) _____

_____ by (date) _____

Signed: _____ Date: _____

Signed: _____ Date: _____

Witnessed by: _____ Date: _____

BOOK THREE

Family and Values

CHAPTER SEVEN — PERSONAL INTEGRITY

LESSON ONE — Values and Role Models

The line below represents your life. Write the date you were born on the line directly below *Date of Birth*. Then write today's date directly under *Now*. On the line between *Date of Birth* and *Now*, write the dates of significant events that have happened in your life, making a note of what each event was. (Example, 1990, won the City Basketball Tournament). Also make a note of a person who was instrumental in making that event special. Do not write anything under *Distant Future*. We will do that later.

Date of Birth　　　　　　　　　　　　　　**Now**　　　　**Distant**
　(Date)　　　　　　　　　　　　　　　　　　(Date)　　　**Future**

_____

Who are some of your role models or the people who influence your life the most?

_____

_____

What are some things you have learned from these people?

_____

_____

What values do you have now that are a result of your past relationships and experiences?

_____

_____

LESSON TWO — Beliefs and Behaviors

Write the definition of values as established by your class:

Values are _____

Complete the lists below. As you think of the people you value, think of the qualities that they possess that cause you to value them. (You may want to refer to your "Important People Tree.")

PEOPLE I VALUE: (3)   **REASONS I VALUE THAT PERSON:**

_____   _____

                                _____

                                _____

_____   _____

                                _____

                                _____

_____   _____

THINGS I VALUE: (3)   **REASONS I VALUE THOSE THINGS:**

_____   _____

                                _____

                                _____

_____   _____

                                _____

                                _____

_____   _____

PRINCIPLES I VALUE: (3)   ## REASONS I VALUE THOSE PRINCIPLES:

_____

_____

_____

_____

_____

_____

_____

_____

_____

_____

_____

_____

_____

_____

_____

Interview a person from your "Important People Tree" on page 41. Record his/her responses below.

Values are . . . .

Complete the lists below. As you think of the people you value, think of the qualities they possess that cause you to value them. You may want to refer to your "Important People Tree."

PEOPLE I VALUE: (3)   ## REASONS I VALUE THAT PERSON:

_____

_____

_____

_____

_____

_____

_____

_____

_____

THINGS I VALUE: (3)   **REASONS I VALUE THOSE THINGS:**

_____

_____

_____

_____

_____

_____

_____

_____

_____

_____

_____

_____

PRINCIPLES I VALUE: (3)   **REASONS I VALUE THOSE PRINCIPLES:**

_____

_____

_____

_____

_____

_____

_____

_____

_____

_____

_____

_____

LESSON THREE — Values Survey

Read the statements below and decide which column matches your feelings about that statement. In the appropriate column, enter 15 if your answer is *very true*, enter 10 if your answer is *sometimes true*, enter 5 if your answer is *not sure*, and enter 0 if your answer if *not true*. Enter only one score per statement.

Interests and Values Survey

	Very True (15)	Sometimes True (10)	Not Sure (5)	Not True (0)
1. I like being the person in charge of a group.		10		
2. I like watching educational programs on TV.		10		
3. Taking risks makes me feel stressed.		10		
4. I want to decide when I clean my room and do my homework.	15			
5. It is more important to make a lot of money than to enjoy the job I am doing.		10		
6 I would rather own an expensive new bike than take piano lessons.			5	
7. I like reading so I can know more about things.			5	
8. I would rather spend time with my friends than go to a museum with my family.		10		
9. I hope to be a movie or TV star someday.			5	
10. When I grow up I want to travel to Europe and China.	15			
11. Eating dinner with my family is important to me.	15			
12. I like learning something new.	15			
13. Someday I would like to be the president of my class.			5	

	Very True (15)	Sometimes True (10)	Not Sure (5)	Not True (0)
14. My friends are more important than my allowance.	15			
15. I like the feelings I have when I achieve something successfully.	15			
16. I would not help someone cheat on a test, even if they paid me a lot of money.	15			
17. If I were on the track team, I would want to be the captain.			5	
18. Being able to buy anything I want would be the best thing about being a grown up.		10		
19. Someday I would like to be able to help people who are less fortunate than I.	15			
20. I think it's important to understand and appreciate music and art.	15			
21. Being able to travel anywhere I want would be the best thing about being a wealthy person.	15			
22. I enjoy making something myself.	15			
23. I often take chances and I enjoy the feelings I have when I do.	15			
24. I try to learn something new every day.	15			
25. When I grow up I want to own a lot of property.	15			
26. When I get something new, I often think, I could make that myself.		10		
27. Someday I want to be famous.	15			
28. I enjoy helping raise money for organizations that help underprivileged children.	15			
29. Whenever I receive money for a gift, I save some of it.	15			
30. If someone offered to give me the answers to a test, I would refuse them.		10		
31. I like to go to movies with my friends.	15			

	Very True (15)	Sometimes True (10)	Not Sure (5)	Not True (0)
32. I don't like it when my parents tell me what to do to help around the house; I would rather think of the chores I want to do myself.	15			
33. I think it's a bad investment to buy a lottery ticket.		10		
34. It's more important to work with people I can talk to every day than to work in a job where I would work alone.	15			
35. Someday I want to be my own boss.	15			
36. It's important to be recognized for things I do well.	15			
37. I would rather visit the Grand Canyon than go to a football game.	15			
38. I like to give my opinions and I get upset when people won't listen to me.	15			
39. I get bored if I am not doing something.	15			
40. It's OK to break a rule if doing so will help someone who really needs help.	15			
41. When I grow up I want to have a lot of money.	15			
42. I think it's more important to spend tax dollars on parks and museums than on building a shelter for homeless people.				0
43. I think it would be fun to be an inventor.	15			
44. When I see a beautiful sunset I want to take a picture of it.	15			
45. When I do something wrong I feel guilty.	15			
46. Sometimes I feel afraid that people won't like me.			5	
47. I would rather take an easier class if it means I can get a good grade than take a more difficult class if it means I might get an average grade.		10		

	Very True (15)	Sometimes True (10)	Not Sure (5)	Not True (0)
48. People who have a lot of money are happier than people who have average incomes.			5	
49. My friends know they can talk to me about their problems and I enjoy helping them.	15			
50. When I think of going on a vacation I think of doing something adventurous.	15			
51. When I grow up I will spend more time with my family than I will spend working.	15			
52. I want to be able to visit all of the states in the country in my lifetime.	15			
53. I would rather work in a job where I am already established than accept a higher paying job where I may have to prove myself.		10		
54. I would rather give a gift I have made than one I have purchased.		10		
55. I enjoy spending time with my parents and I can tell them how I feel.	15			
56. I think I am creative.	15			
57. If I won $1,000, I would spend the money to travel.	15			
58 When I learn something new, it is fun!	15			
59. I often think about what I could do to help people who are experiencing hard times.	15			
60. I often feel upset when someone tells me what to do.		10		
61. It is more important to feel good about the quality of my work than it is to please others.		10		
62. I think it would be fun to serve on a jury so I could make sure people pay for the crimes.		10		
63. I want to have my own family when I grow up.	15			
64. I would like to know how computers work.		10		
65. I like activities that I can do with my friends.	15			

	Very True (15)	Sometimes True (10)	Not Sure (5)	Not True (0)
66. When people want my help, I feel good.	15			
67. Family time is important to me.	15			
68. I can't imagine being single all of my life.	15			
69. I like to spend my own money to fix up my room.	15			
70. I would like to have my picture in the newspaper.	15			
71. I like to decide things for myself.	15			
72. Someday I would like to be famous.	15			
73. I would rather live where I do now than move to a new city and go to a new school.	15			
74. I spend some of my free time doing creative things with music or art.	15			
75. I would rather go to a restaurant that I like than go to a new restaurant.		10		
76. I believe families should be close.	15			
77. Being consistent is more important than trying new methods.		10		
78. I would spend the summer with a relative I have never met.			5	
79. Working as a volunteer is rewarding.	15			
80. I would spend my money for a work of art.	15			
81. If my friends are doing something that I think is wrong, I will go home.			5	
82. I think I would like to learn to write music or poetry.	15			
83. I enjoy learning about historical events.		10		
84. Going to parties is a worthwhile use of my time.	15			
85. I think people should know about it when I do something I am proud of.	15			

	Very True (15)	Sometimes True (10)	Not Sure (5)	Not True (0)
86. I would like to learn mountain climbing.	15			
87. Someday I would like to see my name in the history books.	15			
88. When the teachers ask for tutors to help younger students, I usually volunteer.	15			
89. I enjoy playing games that help me learn facts.		10		
90. I enjoy visiting art museums more than shopping or sports.			5	
91. Someday I want to be rich enough to buy the most expensive car.		10		
92. I would like to learn to sail a boat.	15			
93. I think I am good at making things.	15			
94. My family is important to me.	15			
95. I would rather live simply than have a lot of things to take care of.		10		
96. If I were a member of the school newspaper, I would want to be the editor.		10		
97. I would like to be able to buy the most expensive shoes and clothes.		10		
98. Taking care of needy people is everyone's responsibility.		10		
99. I have good organizational skills.	15			
100. I would like to be chosen as the most popular student in my school.	15			
101. It is important for family members to talk to each other about their feelings.	15			
102. I would rather do a task by myself than with other people.			5	
103. Knowledge is power.	15			
104. I would rather be the principal than just a teacher.		10		

On the line next to each number listed below, write the numerical value you gave to the response you selected for the corresponding statement. For example, if you entered number 10 under the *Not Sure* column for statement number 11, you will enter number 10 on line number 11 below. When you have completed entering all of the numbers, total each of the columns below.

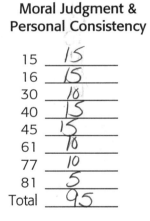

Family
11	15
51	15
55	15
63	15
67	15
76	15
94	15
101	15
Total	120

Adventure
10	15
12	5
21	15
23	15
39	15
78	5
86	15
92	15
Total	110

Creativity
22	15
26	10
43	15
54	10
56	15
74	15
82	15
93	15
Total	50

Power
1	10
13	5
17	5
38	15
62	10
96	10
99	15
104	10
Total	80

Moral Judgment & Personal Consistency
15	15
16	15
30	10
40	15
45	15
61	10
77	10
81	5
Total	95

Recognition
9	5
27	15
36	15
70	15
72	15
85	15
87	15
100	15
Total	110

Knowledge
2	10
7	5
24	15
58	15
64	10
83	10
89	10
103	15
Total	90

Money or Wealth
5	10
6	5
18	10
25	15
41	15
48	5
91	10
97	10
Total	80

Friendship & Companionship
8	10
14	15
31	15
34	15
46	5
65	15
68	15
84	15
Total	105

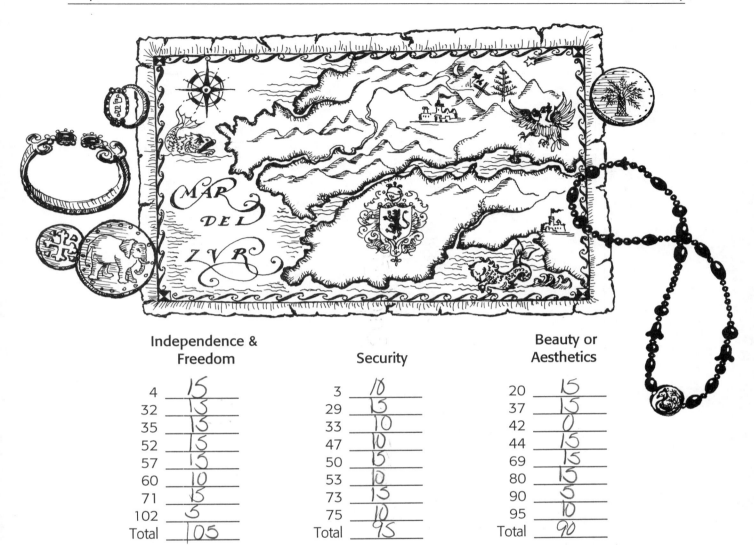

Independence & Freedom

4	15
32	15
35	15
52	15
57	15
60	10
71	15
102	5
Total	105

Security

3	10
29	15
33	10
47	10
50	15
53	10
73	15
75	10
Total	95

Beauty or Aesthetics

20	15
37	15
42	0
44	15
69	15
80	15
90	5
95	10
Total	90

Helping Others

19	15
28	15
49	15
59	15
66	15
79	15
88	15
98	10
Total	115

Now, enter the categories and the score for each category *in order,*
listing the category with the highest score first, the category with
the next highest score second, etc.

Category:	Score:
family	120
helping others	115
adventure	110
recognition	110
friendship	105
independance	105
moral	95
security	95
knowledge	90
beauty/aesthetics	90
power	80
money	80
creativity	50

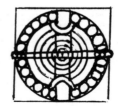

This exercise is adapted from *Choices,* Copyright Girls Incorporated of Greater Santa Barbara,
Advocacy Press, Santa Barbara, CA 1983.

Read the descriptions of the categories for which your scores ranked number *one*, number *two* and number *three*. These are the areas which more than likely reflect your values at the present time. Remember, though, you are still developing your decision-making skills. If you take this survey again in a few years, you may find that your interests have changed.

Family

Someone with a very high score in this category greatly values the closeness of relationships. Parents and children feel close to each other and spend time together. *Family* can also mean other persons or friends who are close to you, if you choose not to join a traditional family. Your inner circle of acquaintances is important. You are a people person. If you score high in this area, you will want a job that allows you plenty of time to enjoy family and friends. Your work hours should be consistent and predictable. You may enjoy a career in counseling, child care, or elder care. You probably would not be happy as a traveling sales representative, an airline pilot or a data entry person who works alone.

Adventure

Careers that allow you to travel may be just right for you if *adventure* was one of your high-ranking categories. You will probably want to experience a certain degree of risk in your career. A job which depends upon the routine completion of daily tasks and a rigid schedule would more than likely seem boring to you. You will want a lot of variety and excitement in your job! Tour guides, flight attendants, fishermen, police officers and fire fighters would probably fall under this category. Do people who want adventure make effective spouses and parents? You would need a spouse and children who understand and accept your need for adventure, but it's not impossible to have both!

Knowledge

For people who rate high in this category, learning is a lifetime event. Some examples of careers for people who value *knowledge* are teaching, research, journalism, and museum work. You probably enjoy reading and watching educational programs on television, and your passion for knowledge can be fulfilled during your non-work hours as well as in your career.

Power

You have the ability to sell your ideas, and other people respect you and follow you. Assuming leadership roles is a "natural" for you and you enjoy facilitating change and seeing your goals accomplished. People who value *power* often have a goal to become the head of an organization. While you may not be able to assume a power position immediately, you are the kind of person who will work extra hours and assume more responsibility to receive promotions to higher levels in an organization. You may also want to start your own business in which you are the boss. People who enjoy power are often involved in politics.

Moral Judgment and Personal Consistency

You are the kind of employee who will focus on the laws and policies which govern society and the workplace. You may find yourself working for a non-profit organization which is in line with your personal values. For instance, if you are concerned about the environment, you may be involved in an organization which recycles paper and other disposable products. You may also become a community volunteer who serves an organization which helps people, if that is your interest.

Friendship and Companionship

Working with others in a team environment will work well for you if friendship and companionship are your strong suit. You are outgoing and people enjoy being with you. Spending time with your friends and family is important to you, so you will want a job which allows for personal time. You may want to think of a job that allows flexibility in scheduling your work hours. Some examples are private counseling, sales, public relations, business consulting, and public service.

Recognition

You thrive on being noticed by other people. You want to be recognized for your abilities and your talents. You will work hard to develop your talents so that you stand out from the rest. Not everyone who falls into this category is a famous movie star or musical talent. You may enjoy being a local radio or television personality. Often people who fall into this category find ways to be a star in their own work environment or community. Who are some of the stand-outs in your school?

Money or Wealth

The amount you earn is the primary motivator when this is your highest scoring category. You will want to work hard in school so you can qualify for jobs which pay the highest salaries. Often these careers require many years of education and hard work. They usually begin to pay off in middle age. If *money and wealth* is your first category, you will want to be sure you think of how you can balance your other interests while you are devoting the next several years to your education and career development.

Independence

You will want to be able to set your own hours if *independence* is your highest value because you probably won't do well in a job that has a rigid work schedule. You could find the flexibility you need in real estate or insurance sales. Some people who work on a free-lance basis are consultants, painting contractors, designers, plumbers, hair stylists, writers and musicians. Those who value independence will want to have the freedom to approach their work when and how they choose!

Security

People who desire security have traditionally held positions in government and well-established corporations. Some examples are the telephone companies, postal service, electronics manufacturers, and the aeronautics industry. However, due to a changing economy, even those jobs have been less secure in recent years. If you value *security* be sure you have a good education and a variety of skills. People who continue to educate themselves and receive up-to-date training in their job skills have a better chance of securing a new job if they are laid off.

Creativity

Creativity is a skill that is used in many career fields. Decorating homes, designing buildings and landscapes, drawing, painting, writing, are all forms of creativity. *Creativity* is required in jobs that involve problem solving and planning also. Highly creative individuals are valued employees when their skills are focused on the work at hand.

Aesthetics

Do you enjoy beautiful people, places and things? If so, you will be happier working in a setting that is pleasing to the eye. Your work environment is almost as important to you as the work you are doing. Try matching your skills with this value. Perhaps you would like to be a hair designer or an art dealer. Or, you may enjoy a job in the out-of-doors as a horticulturist or park ranger.

Helping Others

If you enjoy making others happy, you will be attracted to one of many positions in the service industry. You could be a recreation director, a youth worker, an activities director in a rehabilitation hospital, a psychologist, a physical therapist, or a sales person. The options in this field are unlimited! You will want to feel appreciated by those you help.

LESSON FOUR — Values as Guides

Lara wants a new watch. She asked each of her parents, who are divorced, to buy it for her. Her dad said to have her mother buy it from the child support payments he gives her. Her mom said to ask her dad because he doesn't give them enough money to buy a watch. Lara doesn't want to be caught in the middle of her parents' arguments, so she decides to steal the watch and tell each parent that the other one bought it for her.

Mike wants to have a "stripe" cut in his hair. All of the guys on the track team are having it done by one of the mothers who is a beautician. Mike asks his mom if it's OK and she says, "No way! This is your senior year and I don't want our relatives and friends to see you that way on graduation day." The night before the track meet Mike has his hair cut. On the day of the meet, his mom sees the stripe on his nearly-shaved head.

Norma's best friend, Monique, told her that she really likes Todd. Norma likes Todd, too, but her friendship with Monique is more important to her. When Todd asks her to go out she tells him, "I'm busy that night, but I think Monique might be interested in going with you."

Tony's dad wants him to go on a camping and fishing trip with him. Tony doesn't really like to fish, but it's his dad's favorite sport. Tony explains this to his dad and asks if there is something else they could do that they might both enjoy. They decide to go backpacking instead.

Ben hasn't seen or talked to his mother for years. She left the family when he was only three years old and now he is fifteen! He is curious about her, but he is also very angry because she has not shown any interest in Ben or his sisters. His mother has cancer and she wants to make peace with her family. Ben doesn't think it's his problem and he refuses to see his mom.

LESSON FIVE — Choosing a Friend

Listed below are descriptions of seven teenagers. Rank in order with #1 being the person you would most likely choose for your best friend, #7 being last. Think about the qualities they possess that made you choose them first or last. Now rank the other individuals 2-6.

Bossie Beatrice   She is quite a leader. She is always telling everyone what to do and how to do it.

\# _____

Positive or Negative Qualities: _____

Helpful Hannah   She is always there to give anyone and everyone a helping hand. She always does it with a smile.

\# _____

Positive or Negative Qualities: _____

Fearless Frank   He's the daredevil of the group. He is always doing exciting things and encouraging everyone else to do so too. He really is funny and fun to be around.

\# _____

Positive or Negative Qualities: _____

Popular Penelope She is beautiful and popular. She is not very friendly with people who aren't in her crowd even though she's the homecoming queen.

\# _____

Positive or Negative Qualities: _____

Smart Sam   Sam is a genius! He makes straight As. Even though his studies
come first, he's a pretty regular guy and friendly, too.

\# _____
Positive or Negative Qualities: _____

Bully Bart   Bart is always pushing people around. He cuts in line and then
threatens you if you complain. He is always looking for a fight.

\# _____
Positive or Negative Qualities: _____

Creative Cathy   Everything that Cathy wears matches. She doesn't even think of
going out of the house unless her hair looks perfect. She helps
the teacher with the bulletin boards and is very concerned about
the way things look in the classroom.

\# _____
Positive or Negative Qualities: _____

Qualities That Are Important to Me!

List the five qualities you consider most important in

SAME SEX FRIEND	OPPOSITE SEX FRIEND	TYPE OF PERSON YOU WOULD CHOOSE AS A MATE
1. _____	1. _____	1. _____
2. _____	2. _____	2. _____
3. _____	3. _____	3. _____
4. _____	4. _____	4. _____
5. _____	5. _____	5. _____

What's the Most Important Quality a Person Can Have?

Girls Say About Guys

Good, great or awesome personality	38%
Honesty/sincerity	12%
Sense of humor	8%
Caring personality	5%
Sensitivity/tenderness	4%

Guys Say About Girls

Good, great or awesome personality	39%
Good looks	10%
Sense of humor	8%
Honesty/sincerity	6%
Intelligence	5%

Results of a national survey taken by *Seventeen* magazine:
(Love & Sex in the '90s: November, 1991)

Qualities That Are Important to Me!

List the five qualities you consider most important in

SAME SEX FRIEND	OPPOSITE SEX FRIEND	TYPE OF PERSON YOU WOULD CHOOSE AS A MATE
1. _____	1. _____	1. _____
2. _____	2. _____	2. _____
3. _____	3. _____	3. _____
4. _____	4. _____	4. _____
5. _____	5. _____	5. _____

LESSON SIX — Congruency

Read the statement below and decide whether you *strongly agree, agree,* are *neutral* or *unsure, disagree* or *strongly disagree* with the statement as written.

	SA	A	N	D	SD
Education is not really that important because many successful people didn't go to school.					
Smoking marijuana is OK because it should be legalized anyway.					
Everyone is joyriding these days. People should expect to have their cars stolen; that's why they have insurance.					
Getting an education is the best way to assure a positive future.					
Having a baby wouldn't be so difficult; there are lots of people to help you take care of a baby.					
If a pregnancy results from sexual activity, the male is equally responsible for the care and support of the baby.					
If you are high or drunk when you engage in risky sexual activities, you shouldn't be held responsible.					
Television is responsible for most of the increase in violence.					
It's OK for a guy to have sex with a girl if she is drunk.					
Sharing homework is OK because what is really important is that we learn the information.					
Capital punishment should not be permitted in our country.					
Juveniles should not be permitted to carry a gun except for a legal purpose when accompanied by an adult.					
All semi-automatic guns should be banned.					

	SA	A	N	D	SD
Health care should be provided for every citizen.					
Welfare recipients should complete community service for their payments.					
Parents should be held responsible for their children's actions.					
Our country should not spend so much money on foreign aid.					
Convicted criminals should lose all their rights.					
In our country today, a criminal's rights are more important than the victim's.					

CHAPTER EIGHT — PERSONAL AND FAMILY RELATIONS

LESSON ONE — The Changing American Family

In the space provided below complete the following statements:

WHAT FAMILY MEANS TO ME:

_____

_____

_____

_____

_____

WHAT FAMILY PROVIDES FOR ME:

_____

_____

_____

_____

_____

WHAT I WANT TO PROVIDE AS A PARENT:

_____

_____

_____

_____

_____

In the space below compare a TV family of the '50s, '60s, or '70s with a TV family today:

Yesterday's Family: _____ Decade: _____

Describe the family _____

_____

_____

_____

Positive qualities: Negative qualities:

_____   _____

_____   _____

_____   _____

_____   _____

Today's Family: _____ Decade: _____

Describe the family _____

_____

_____

_____

Positive qualities: Negative qualities:

_____   _____

_____   _____

_____   _____

_____   _____

A Bill of Rights for Children

We believe that every child has the following rights:

- To be wanted and planned for by the parents.

- To be reared by parents who have been trained in the skills of parenting.

- To be provided with the best possible environment in which to grow and develop in the uterus of the mother. (This refers to the period between conception and the actual birth.)

- To be provided with the proper nutrition. (This also applies to the nutrition of the mother during the period of pregnancy.)

- To be protected against injuries, to the extent that they can be prevented by reasonable care and foresight.

- To live in an uncrowded, peaceful, clean, secure home.

- To have clean clothing, suitably adapted to the weather, and adequate sanitary facilities.

- To receive warm, loving, patient and skillful care by the parents.

- To receive a large number and variety of learning experiences, including opportunities to explore the environment within reasonable limits.

- To receive proper immunizations at the appropriate times.

- To be protected against abuse and neglect. If parents cannot or will not meet reasonable standards in this respect, then the agencies of society must step in to do whatever is necessary to correct the mistreatment.

The United Nations Declaration on the Rights of the Child also includes the following rights in addition to the ones we have listed:

- A name and nationality.

- Special care if handicapped.

- To be among the first to receive relief in time of disaster.

- To learn to be useful members of society.

- To be brought up in a spirit of peace and universal brotherhood.

- To enjoy all of these rights, regardless of race, color, sex, religion, national or social origin.

- To receive good medical care.

- To attend a good school at the proper age, and to receive the instruction and motivation that, together with other life experiences, will help each individual to develop to the limits of his or her innate capabilities.

This exercise is adapted from Gordon, Sol & Wollin, Mina "Parenting," Oxford Book Company, Inc., New York, NY, 1983 p. 28.

LESSON TWO — The Many Roles of a Parent

List in order below the roles of a parent that you feel are the most important to the least important. Next to each of those roles list the corresponding responsibilities.

Roles of a Parent   Responsibilities of that Role

_____

_____

_____

_____   _____

_____

_____

_____   _____

_____

_____

_____   _____

_____

_____

_____   _____

_____

_____

_____   _____

_____

LESSON THREE — Teen Fathers Count and Should Be Counted

Read the statement below and decide whether you *strongly agree, agree,* are *neutral* or *unsure, disagree* or *strongly disagree* with the statement as written.

Statements:

	SA	A	N	D	SD
Teenage fathers who do not marry the mother want to avoid the responsibility of parenting.					
Teenage mothers should not have to be totally responsible for their child's care and upbringing.					
Teenage fathers have as many problems with parenting as teenage mothers.					
Teenage mothers have more power than teenage fathers over their children.					
The kind of parent a person becomes depends upon the kind of parent the person had.					
Teenage fathers are not marrying their children's mothers, due to the lack of employment and resultant income to provide for the family.					
In today's society it is accepted that teenage fathers are NOT responsible for the children they father.					
Most teenage fathers want to care for the children they father.					

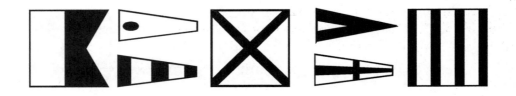

LESSON FOUR — Parenting Requires Sacrifice

Below are some Case Studies that involve individuals who are faced with making some sacrifices because they are parents. As you read the Case Studies, think about how the sacrifices would affect the parent(s), the child, and maybe even society now and in the future.

Terrance and Sophie have been married for six months. Terrance works at a local service station and is a high school dropout. Sophie has just entered her junior year in high school and is going to have a baby in November. Terrance and Sophie have agreed that she will drop out of school to take care of the baby. Now Sophie has decided that she wants to try to finish the semester by completing her work at home and return to school in January. Terrance is concerned about the effect it will have on the baby if Sophie isn't at home all the time.

Darren and Ellie are fifteen and have been dating for six months when Ellie finds out she is pregnant. Ellie wants to have an abortion and Darren wants her to have the baby. He says that it is his baby too and that she doesn't have a right to have an abortion if he doesn't want her to. Comment on the following options:

- ◆ Ellie agrees to have the baby and put it up for adoption. She says if Darren wants the baby his parents can adopt it.

- ◆ Ellie says she doesn't care what Darren wants. It is her body and she can do whatever she wants.

- ◆ Ellie says she will have the baby if Darren marries her and drops out of school so he can support her and the baby.

Clarissa is sixteen years old and has a 12-month old baby. She used to be very popular and go out a lot but now she has very few friends. She has the sole responsibility for her baby and has no one to help her. She would like to go out once in a while but her friends do not like it when she brings the baby along. She doesn't trust anyone else to care for her baby so she doesn't have a baby sitter. She also doesn't have any extra money to pay a sitter.

Sheila and Dave are married and they are both still in school. Sheila wants to have a baby now because she wants to have a big family, so she thinks they should get started. Dave wants to go on to college and wants Sheila to think about it too. He says they will be better able to support a big family if they both get an education. He also still likes to party and even though he is married he is not sure he is responsible enough to be a parent.

Tara was an honor student and looking forward to going to college. She was sure she would get a scholarship to the university because not only were her grades outstanding but she was also a member of the student council, on the varsity volleyball and track teams, and a member of the debate team. She was also very active in her community as a volunteer at the hospital and a member of Teen Town Hall. She recently found out that she is pregnant. She has spoken with several people and has received the following advice:

- Have the baby and put it up for adoption.
- Have the baby, keep it, and get her GED. Then she can go right to work.
- Have an abortion.

What Would You Do?

In the space below, write a paragraph about how your life would change if you found out today that you were going to become a parent this year. Remember both males and females become parents even though just females become pregnant. Be sure to include how you would feel, who you would talk with, what you would do, what sacrifices you would have to make.

_____

_____

_____

_____

_____

_____

_____

_____

_____

_____

_____

_____

_____

LESSON FIVE — Financial Responsibility

How much do you know about the cost of raising a child? What are some of the costs a parent needs to consider?

Below are a few of the major items. Add any others to the list that you and your classmates think are necessary. Then estimate the cost of that item for *one year*.

Medical Expenses:	Before birth	$ _____
	Birth	$ _____
	First year	$ _____
Equipment:	Bassinet	$ _____
	Bed	$ _____
	Changing table	$ _____
	Car seat	$ _____
	Stroller	$ _____
	High chair	$ _____
	Rocking chair	$ _____
	Bottles	$ _____
	Dishes/spoons	$ _____
Clothing		$ _____
Diapers		$ _____
Food		$ _____
Supplies	Soap	$ _____
	Shampoo	$ _____
	Lotion	$ _____
	Powder	$ _____
	Paper products	$ _____
Day Care		$ _____
Baby sitters		$ _____
Photographs		$ _____

Below add any others that you think are important.

_____ $ _____

_____ $ _____

_____ $ _____

_____ $ _____

                                                   $ _____

LESSON SIX — Child Growth and Development

In the space below, write a short paragraph to complete the following sentence:

"I think being a responsible parent means. . . . "

_____

_____

_____

_____

_____

_____

_____

_____

_____

_____

LESSONS SEVEN TO ELEVEN — Stages of Development

List the three most important needs of a child in each stage of development. Also list the three most important roles or responsibilities a parent has to the child during that stage of development.

INFANCY

Needs of Child

_____

_____

_____

Roles/Responsibilities of a Parent

_____

_____

_____

TODDLER

Needs of Child

_____

_____

_____

Roles/Responsibilities of a Parent

_____

_____

_____

PRESCHOOLER

Needs of Child

_____

_____

_____

Roles/Responsibilities of a Parent

_____

_____

_____

PRIMARY YEARS

Needs of Child

_____

_____

_____

Roles/Responsibilities of a Parent

_____

_____

_____

MIDDLE YEARS

Needs of Child

_____

_____

_____

Roles/Responsibilities of a Parent

_____

_____

_____

LESSON TWELVE — Communication

In the space below list what kind of sounds an infant might respond to positively.

_____

Negatively? _____

What kinds of touch would an infant respond to positively?

_____

Negatively? _____

Read the Case Studies below and decide how the parent could respond to the child using effective communication skills.

Susie is two years old. She has learned that screaming gets attention. She is in the grocery store with her father and wants a box of animal crackers. As her father goes down the aisle where the animal crackers are located, Susie begins screaming at the top of her lungs. You're Susie's dad. How would you communicate with her?

José is 10 months old. He has decided that he wants to feed himself all the time. At dinner time for the last three days, after a few bites of food, José has taken his bowl and dumped it over his head. You are José's mom and you are ready to give him his dinner. What would you say?

Kenya and her twin brother Kyle are always playing together. They are five years old. Most of the time they play very nicely but today they have been bickering all day. You have listened to them argue off and on all day. They start at it again. What would you say to them?

Kwan is eighteen months old. She has the chicken pox and is having a hard time going to sleep. She's crying softly in her bed. What would you say and do?

Clarence, your two and a half year old son, always seems to be underfoot at dinner time. You are Clarence's dad and you really would like him to take his toys to the other side of the room where you could see him but he wouldn't be right under your feet. You speak to him and he moves to the other side of the room. In about five minutes, he's right back under your feet. What do you say now?

Trashon is out in the back yard. She is four years old and is a real handful. She can always seem to find something to climb on or over. As you look out the door you see her balancing herself on several boxes she has stacked up and she is just about to go over the fence. What do you say and do?

LESSON THIRTEEN — Discipline or Punishment

EFFECTIVE **Ds** FOR DISCIPLINE!

In the space provided below, list at least three ways that you could DIFFUSE anger in a situation when disciplining a child was required. Note: One might not always be angry when discipline was necessary; however, diffusing anger should always be the first step if a person is angry. If not angry, the parent or person in authority would move to the second step.

DIFFUSE anger: One should remain firm—but show firmness with fairness. Disciplining when angry usually results in punishment.

1. _____

2. _____

3. _____

Below are listed three scenarios which might occur with children. Read the scenario and

DEFINE problem: Use "I Messages" to state how you feel about the behavior and what you want to have happen. If the situation were real you would also want to use reflective listening to hear the child's point of view.

DISCOVER alternatives: Through effective communication list acceptable alternatives to the behavior that is unacceptable while treating the child with dignity and respect as you maintain your own dignity.

DECIDE on consequences: Consequences should be structured and logical. They should make sense to the child.

DELIVER the results: What was the behavior that was unacceptable?

♦ What could the child do differently in the future?

♦ What could the parent do differently in the future?

♦ What is the shared expectation? (Do you both understand what is expected in the future?)

♦ Set the standards clearly so the child will know what to expect (consequences) if the behavior is repeated.

Put Yourself in the Parent Seat!

Four-year old Amy has been at day care all day and hasn't had a nap. She is tired and cranky when her mom Maria picks her up. Maria is tired, but she needs to make dinner, do the wash, and study for a test she has at school the next day. She asks Amy to play with her dolls on her bed. (Maria thought she might fall asleep for a nap if she played quietly.) Maria started dinner and went to check on Amy. Amy had crawled out of bed, gone in the bathroom and gotten into Maria's makeup. She had drawn on the walls with Maria's lipstick. Maria was livid! You are Maria.

DEFINE PROBLEM:(USE "I MESSAGES") I feel _____

when you _____

I want _____

DISCOVER and share alternatives to the unacceptable behavior. What could the child have done differently?

_____

_____

DECIDE on consequences. Be sure they are fair, firm, logical, and can be clearly understood by the child. Remember the goal is to teach rather than to punish.

_____

_____

DELIVER results: Will the above accomplish a change in behavior? Think about the following questions:

- What was the behavior that was unacceptable?
- What could the child do differently in the future?
- What could the parent do differently in the future?
- What do you think is the shared expectation? (Do you both understand what is expected in the future?)
- Were the standards set clearly so the child will know what to expect (consequences) if the behavior is repeated?

Manuel, five, and Carlos, seven, were playing outside. It had been raining and there were lots of puddles. Their mom Tricia asked them not to play in the puddles or get dirty because they were supposed to go to Grandma's for dinner in about thirty minutes. The boys got bored and pretty soon were playing in the puddles, splashing each other and having a lot of fun. When Tricia called out to tell them to come in for it was time to leave, she could not believe the mess she saw! You are Tricia.

DEFINE PROBLEM: (USE "I MESSAGES") I feel _____

when you _____

I want _____

DISCOVER and share alternatives to the unacceptable behavior. What could the children have done differently?

_____

_____

DECIDE on consequences. Be sure they are fair, firm, logical, and can be clearly understood by the children. Remember the goal is to teach rather than to punish.

_____

_____

DELIVER results: Will the above accomplish a change in behavior? Think about the following questions:

- What was the behavior that was unacceptable?
- What could the children do differently in the future?
- What could the parent do differently in the future?
- What do you think is the shared expectation? (Do all of you understand what is expected in the future?)
- Were the standards set clearly so the children will know what to expect (consequences) if the behavior is repeated?

Derrick was riding with his dad, Jerome, on Saturday in his delivery truck while Jerome was making his deliveries. Now that Derrick was six, he had convinced Jerome that he was old enough to go along. After about three hours, Derrick got bored and began to whine and complain. They were too far away from home for Jerome to take Derrick home. The whining and complaining got worse and worse. Jerome had had enough! You are Jerome.

DEFINE PROBLEM: (USE "I MESSAGES") I feel _____

when you _____

I want _____

DISCOVER and share alternatives to the unacceptable behavior. What could the child have done differently?

_____

_____

DECIDE on consequences. Be sure they are fair, firm, logical, and can be clearly understood by the child. Remember the goal is to teach rather than to punish.

_____

_____

DELIVER results: Will the above accomplish a change in behavior? Think about the following questions:

- What was the behavior that was unacceptable?
- What could the child do differently in the future?
- What could the parent do differently in the future?
- What do you think is the shared expectation? (Do you both understand what is expected in the future?)
- Were the standards set clearly so the child will know what to expect (consequences) if the behavior is repeated?

LESSON FOURTEEN — Child Abuse and Neglect

You Be the Judge!

Using the techniques we learned yesterday and considering developmental skills, consider the following situations and how they were handled. Which Was It? *Discipline, Punishment,* or *Child Abuse* or *Neglect*? In the space provided, put a D for Discipline, P for Punishment, C for Child Abuse or Neglect.

1. Jenny was late for dinner so her mother sent her to bed without any supper.   _____

2. James beat up his little brother so his dad beat him up.   _____

3. Susie kept throwing her food on the floor. Her mother took her food away, washed her hands and face and said, "I feel disappointed when you throw your food on the floor. I want you to eat your dinner properly. When you are ready to do that let me know and I will return your dinner to you and will expect that you are ready to behave."   _____

4. Jamie squirmed and squirmed when his mother changed his diaper. His mom decided to leave a dirty diaper on him all day to teach him a lesson.   _____

5. Angel always got out of bed at night and wandered around. His dad was tired of it so he locked him in his room.   _____

CHAPTER NINE — PERSONAL HEALTH

LESSON ONE — Wellness and Risks

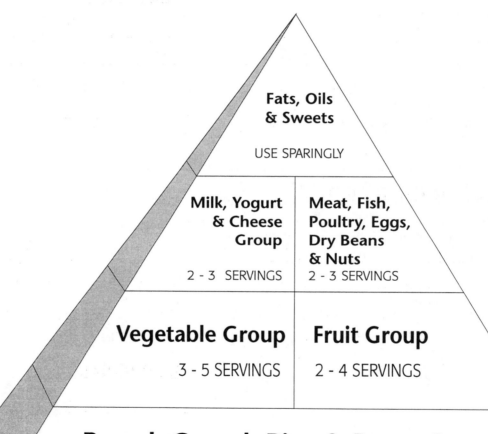

Fats, Oils
& Sweets

USE SPARINGLY

Milk, Yogurt
& Cheese
Group

2 - 3 SERVINGS

Meat, Fish,
Poultry, Eggs,
Dry Beans
& Nuts

2 - 3 SERVINGS

Vegetable Group

3 - 5 SERVINGS

Fruit Group

2 - 4 SERVINGS

Bread, Cereal, Rice & Pasta Group

6 -11 SERVINGS

Personal Health Maintenance Plan:

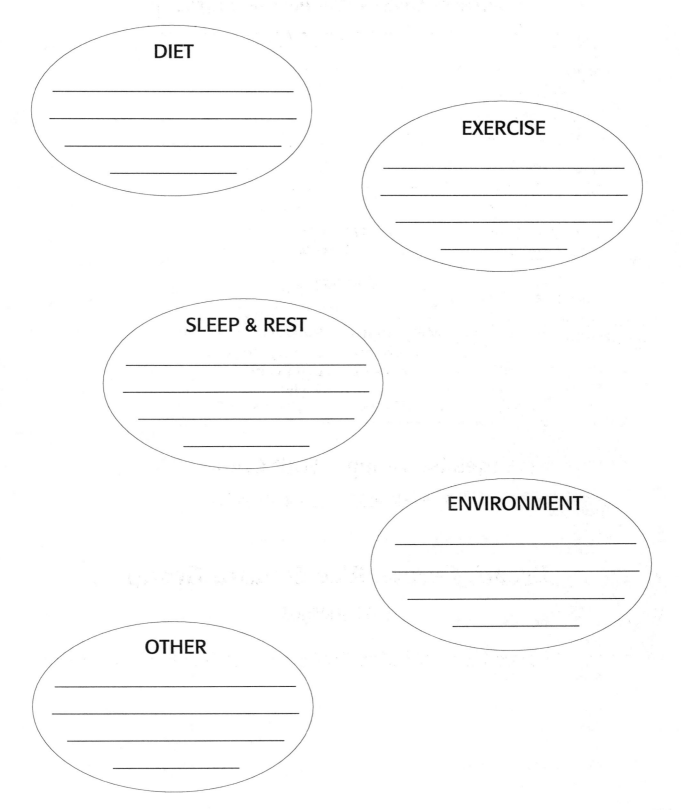

DIET

EXERCISE

SLEEP & REST

ENVIRONMENT

OTHER

LESSON THREE — Communicable Diseases

Causes of Diseases	List at least one disease.
Heredity	_____
Environment	_____
Life style	_____
Germs	_____

Circle whether each of the following behaviors is

		High Risk	Low Risk	No Risk
1.	Smoking a pack of cigarettes a day	HR	LR	NR
2.	Eating one meal a day	HR	LR	NR
3.	Drinking from the same cup as someone who has a cold	HR	LR	NR
4.	Having unprotected sex with anyone	HR	LR	NR
5.	Eating contaminated food	HR	LR	NR
6.	Living in the same house with someone with HIV	HR	LR	NR
7.	Wearing someone's pierced earring	HR	LR	NR
8.	Taking mega doses of vitamins	HR	LR	NR
9.	Taking another person's prescription medicine	HR	LR	NR
10.	Kissing someone you don't know	HR	LR	NR
11.	Drinking three glasses of orange juice every day	HR	LR	NR
12.	Not wearing your seat belt	HR	LR	NR

LESSON FOUR — Personal Hygiene

Personal Hygiene Plan:

LESSON FIVE — Domestic Violence

Read the statement below and decide whether you strongly agree, agree, are neutral or unsure, disagree or strongly disagree with the statement as written.

I BELIEVE THAT. . .

_____ violence is preventable.

_____ a main cause of violence among my peers is due to personal pride.

_____ the police can reduce the amount of violence in my neighborhood.

_____ violence is justified when it comes to self defense.

_____ community members can reduce the amount of violence in my neighborhood.

_____ a main cause of violence among my peers is due to drugs.

_____ I can reduce my risk of becoming a victim of violence.

_____ a main cause of violence among my peers is due to fights over boyfriends/girlfriends.

_____ I can reduce my risk of becoming a victim of homicide.

_____ a main cause of violence among my peers is due to conditions between people who already know each other.

_____ a main cause of violence among my peers is due to the amount of violence in the media or on television.

_____ violence is justified when acting on revenge.

_____ a main cause of violence among my peers is due to fights caused by boyfriends/girlfriends.

_____ violence within families is preventable.

_____ a main cause of violence among my peers is due to the availability of guns.

_____ I am at risk of becoming a victim of homicide.

_____ a person deserves to be physically hurt if he/she provokes it.

_____ a main cause of violence among my peers is due to getting attention between peers.

_____ violence is preventable among my peers.

_____ a main cause of violence among my peers is due to conflicts in
sexual relationships.

_____ I am at risk of becoming a victim of violence.

_____ a main cause of violence among my peers is due to justifiable physical acts
toward a girlfriend/boyfriend.

_____ violence or some kind of physical abuse is expected in sexual relationships.

_____ a main cause of violence among my peers is due to limited ways of
expressing anger.

_____ I have been a victim of violence.

_____ a main cause of violence among my peers is due to not getting enough
attention from their parents.

_____ a solution to violence is to identify positive ways to express anger.

_____ a solution to violence is to diffuse or leave a violent situation.

_____ I can cope with being a victim of violence.

_____ violence is based on a choice in behavior.

_____ I believe student anti-violence education should be provided in schools.

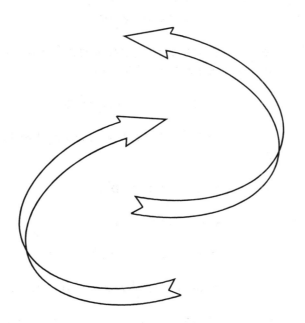

List several concrete things that you can do to decrease your personal risk for violence in your own life and several concrete actions that could be initiated at our school to decrease the potential for violence in our school and community.

PERSONAL VIOLENCE REDUCTION:

_____

_____

_____

_____

VIOLENCE REDUCTION IN OUR SCHOOL:

IDEAS: ACTION STEPS:

LESSON SIX — Personal Safety

Which Is It?

In the space provided after each scenario, write whether it depicts

- ◆ DATE RAPE
- ◆ DATE VIOLENCE
- ◆ SEXUAL HARASSMENT
- ◆ ACCEPTABLE BEHAVIOR
- ◆ UNSURE

After making your decision, list skills an individual in that situation could use to avoid that situation if the behavior is inappropriate.

1. Sammy and Lureen have had intercourse before. Lureen has decided she doesn't want to continue because she is afraid she will get pregnant. She tells Sammy and he becomes very angry and grabs her by the hair. He begins to kiss her and unbutton her blouse.

2. Lureen pulls away and begins to run. Sammy swears at her and threatens to beat her up. The next time Sammy sees Lureen he makes "dirty" comments about her in front of others.

3. Maria really likes José. Every time she sees him she flirts with him. José doesn't seem interested but he is polite. One day when Maria sees José in a crowd of his friends, she grabs his buttocks as she walks by. José is embarrassed as everyone snickers.

4. Every time Leon sees Rachel he tells her how "hot" she is. He is always whistling, winking, sometimes even patting her buttocks when he passes in the hall at school. Rachel thinks Leon is hot too and wishes he would ask her out.

5. Susie and Bill have been dating for a long time. One day they are at home alone at Susie's house and go up to her bedroom and begin to kiss and touch each other's genitals. All of a sudden Susie wants to stop but Bill doesn't listen. Whenever Susie tells him to stop, he kisses her and goes a little further. Soon he is on top of her, she is crying and they have intercourse.

6. Madeline goes to a party with several of her friends. She has a few beers and begins to feel "woozie." Her friends are leaving and want Madeline to go with them but she says she is OK and wants to stay. She starts dancing with Tyrone and has a few more beers. The next morning when she wakes up, she doesn't remember leaving the party or how she got home. A few months later she discovers she has a sexually-transmitted disease.

7. There's a radio call-in show that takes requests. Cheryl is always calling in requesting songs for Mickey. Whenever she sees him at school she flirts with him and says some very risqué things. Mickey likes all the attention. It makes him feel sexy and important.

8. Claudia has a cute figure and wears clothes that compliment her figure, but they are not inappropriate for the dress code at her school. A couple of boys are always making comments about her body and she doesn't like it. She has told them so several times. She doesn't think she should have to stop wearing fashionable clothes to get them to stop making comments.

9. Clark picked up Loretta for a date. As soon as she got in the car he started yelling at her because he heard she had been flirting with Roger. All evening long he was in a bad mood and really grumpy. On the way home they stopped at a place they usually parked to make out. Loretta wasn't in the mood and asked Clark to take her home. He exploded and slapped her hard on the side of the head. The next day she had a bad bruise.

10. Create your own scenario—either real or fictitious. If the situation is real, do not use real names as we may be sharing these in class.

_____

_____

_____

_____

_____

_____

_____

_____

_____

_____

_____

_____

BOOK FOUR
Making Choices

CHAPTER TEN — CAREER PLANNING

LESSON ONE — Choosing a Career

Complete the SKILLS INVENTORY below. Some of the items may have more than one check and some may have none. When you are finished, tally all the checks and record the totals. The sections with the greatest number of checks will indicate your strengths. Look back to page 114 in the workbook and review your Interest & Values Survey. Based on the two surveys, pick three Interest Categories that you feel are the highest combination of your Skills and Interests. These will be recorded on the **BOLD** lines under **INTEREST CATEGORY** on page 161 of the workbook.

	Skills I Currently Possess	Skills I Am Curious About	Skills I Would Like to Be Paid For
PEOPLE SKILLS			
MANAGING			
Leading others	_____	_____	_____
Influencing others	_____	_____	_____
Supervising others	_____	_____	_____
Planning with others	_____	_____	_____
Giving clear directions	_____	_____	_____
Giving recognition	_____	_____	_____
Accepting responsibility for decisions	_____	_____	_____
Giving criticism in a positive manner	_____	_____	_____
Delegating responsibilities	_____	_____	_____
Self-motivating	_____	_____	_____
Willing to initiate action and/or take risks to succeed	_____	_____	_____
Able to make decisions	_____	_____	_____
Other _____	_____	_____	_____
TOTAL SCORE:	_____	_____	_____

	Skills I Currently Possess	Skills I Am Curious About	Skills I Would Like to Be Paid For
HELPING			
Understanding	_____	_____	_____
Caring/sharing	_____	_____	_____
Likes to resolve conflict	_____	_____	_____
Likes being part of a team	_____	_____	_____
Listening to problems	_____	_____	_____
Takes care of children	_____	_____	_____
Takes care of elderly	_____	_____	_____
Sensitive to others' feelings	_____	_____	_____
Peacemaking/negotiating	_____	_____	_____
Other _____	_____	_____	_____
TOTAL SCORE:	_____	_____	_____
TEACHING			
Patient	_____	_____	_____
Encouraging others	_____	_____	_____
Helping others succeed	_____	_____	_____
Speaking to groups	_____	_____	_____
Leading discussions	_____	_____	_____
Giving information	_____	_____	_____
Giving advice	_____	_____	_____
Giving thorough explanations	_____	_____	_____
Other _____	_____	_____	_____
TOTAL SCORE:	_____	_____	_____

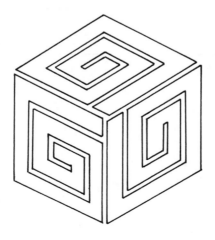

	Skills I Currently Possess	Skills I Am Curious About	Skills I Would Like to Be Paid For
MENTAL SKILLS			
WORKING WITH IDEAS/INFORMATION			
Logical	_____	_____	_____
Curious	_____	_____	_____
Enjoys reading	_____	_____	_____
Gathering information	_____	_____	_____
Observing and comparing	_____	_____	_____
Finding the cause of a problem	_____	_____	_____
Developing ideas and solutions	_____	_____	_____
Predicting outcomes	_____	_____	_____
Able to concentrate	_____	_____	_____
Evaluating results	_____	_____	_____
Other _____	_____	_____	_____
TOTAL SCORE:	_____	_____	_____
WORKING WITH NUMBERS/DETAILS			
Good organizational skills	_____	_____	_____
Good in math	_____	_____	_____
Likes record keeping	_____	_____	_____
Meets deadlines	_____	_____	_____
Good memory for numbers	_____	_____	_____
Attention to detail	_____	_____	_____
Solves problems	_____	_____	_____
Neat, precise	_____	_____	_____
Manages money efficiently	_____	_____	_____
Thinks concretely	_____	_____	_____
Other _____	_____	_____	_____
TOTAL SCORE:	_____	_____	_____

	Skills I Currently Possess	Skills I Am Curious About	Skills I Would Like to Be Paid For
COMMUNICATING IDEAS			
Possesses effective communication skills	_____	_____	_____
Understands non-verbal as well as verbal messages	_____	_____	_____
Listens	_____	_____	_____
Enjoys speaking in front of a group	_____	_____	_____
Likes debating	_____	_____	_____
Likes writing	_____	_____	_____
Has a sense of humor	_____	_____	_____
Tells stories well	_____	_____	_____
Other _____	_____	_____	_____
TOTAL SCORE:	_____	_____	_____

PHYSICAL/CREATIVE SKILLS:

CREATING/PERFORMING:			
Able to draw	_____	_____	_____
Able to paint	_____	_____	_____
Able to write	_____	_____	_____
Able to act	_____	_____	_____
Able to dance	_____	_____	_____
Physically talented	_____	_____	_____
Likes to sing	_____	_____	_____
Able to visualize images, colors, shapes	_____	_____	_____
Sense of space	_____	_____	_____
Other _____	_____	_____	_____
TOTAL SCORE:	_____	_____	_____

	Skills I Currently Possess	Skills I Am Curious About	Skills I Would Like to Be Paid For
WORKING WITH MY HANDS			
Small motor skills (use of hands for detail)	_____	_____	_____
Large motor skills (strength & endurance)	_____	_____	_____
Using small machines	_____	_____	_____
Good hand/eye coordination	_____	_____	_____
Using large machines	_____	_____	_____
Repairing things	_____	_____	_____
Sewing things	_____	_____	_____
Painting things	_____	_____	_____
Building things	_____	_____	_____
Growing things	_____	_____	_____
Working outdoors	_____	_____	_____
Working indoors	_____	_____	_____
Working with crafts	_____	_____	_____
Other _____	_____	_____	_____
TOTAL SCORE:	_____	_____	_____

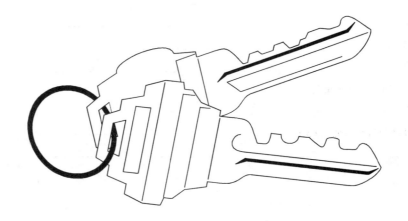

After completing the SKILLS SURVEY look at the three categories for which your scores were highest and record them in column *two*. In column *three* put the three careers which appeal to you that relate to your Interests and Skills. Remember, you need to consider interests, values, and skills as you plan for your future career. Also remember, you may change your mind several times.

Column *four* will be completed during Lesson Two. Columns *five* and *six* will be completed during Lesson Four. You will list the *Skills You Currently Possess* that pertain to the careers you have listed and the *Skills You Need to Acquire* that pertain to that career. At the bottom of the page is a space for *General Skills I Possess* and also a space for your homework assignment.

INTEREST CATEGORY	SKILL CATEGORY	CAREERS	EDUCATIONAL REQUIREMENTS	SKILLS I CURRENTLY POSSESS	SKILLS I NEED TO ACQUIRE
_____	_____	_____	_____	_____	_____
		_____	_____	_____	_____
		_____	_____	_____	_____
_____	_____	_____	_____	_____	_____
		_____	_____	_____	_____
		_____	_____	_____	_____
_____	_____	_____	_____	_____	_____
		_____	_____	_____	_____
		_____	_____	_____	_____

General Skills I Possess:

_____

_____

_____

I think the most interesting career I've listed would be because

_____

_____

_____

_____

LESSON TWO — Non-traditional Career Opportunities

Think of someone in a non-traditional career that you think is very successful and in the space below, write a short paragraph about that person and his/her career choice.

_____

_____

_____

_____

_____

_____

_____

_____

_____

_____

_____

_____

_____

LESSON THREE — Tech Prep and College Prep

Use this page to take notes about the different types of schools in your area that are of interest to you.

Name of school/program: _____

Location: _____

Requirements for admission: _____

_____

Programs offered: _____

_____

Costs: _____

Financial aid available: _____

Other pertinent information: _____

_____

Name of school/program: _____

Location: _____

Requirements for admission: _____

_____

Programs offered: _____

_____

Costs: _____

Financial aid available: _____

Other pertinent information: _____

_____

Name of school/program: _____

Location: _____

Requirements for admission: _____

_____

Programs offered: _____

_____

Costs: _____

Financial aid available: _____

Other pertinent information: _____

_____

LESSON FOUR — Financial Aid

In the space below list at least two resources to find information about Financial Aid.

_____

_____

_____

_____

List at least one person who could help you find out about Financial Aid.

_____

_____

_____

List at least one source of Financial Aid that is available to students who graduate from our school district or in our community.

_____

_____

LESSON FIVE — Job and College Readiness

Below you will see a résumé of a recent high school graduate. The next page is a blank page for you to begin filling in your résumé. Even though you may not have much to put on it now, there is probably more than you think. Perhaps you can complete it using information you hope will be fact by the time you graduate from high school as well as current information. The idea is for you to have some practice writing a résumé.

IMA HARDWORKER

PERMANENT ADDRESS: SCHOOL ADDRESS:
100 ACADEMIC STREET   ACHIEVEMENT HIGH SCHOOL
ANYTOWN, U.S.A.   ANYTOWN, U.S.A.

OBJECTIVE: To receive scholarship to assist with the financial expenses of my education.

EDUCATION:
Achievement High School   Graduated: 1994
                                      G.P.A.: 3.66
Success Middle School   1988-90

WORK EXPERIENCE:
The GAP—Sales Associate   1992-Present
Church Nursery—Childcare   1988-Present
Lawn care(my neighborhood)   1988-1992

ACTIVITIES:
Debate Team   Sept. 92-94
Anytown/Unitown Counselor   June 90-Present
    Cultural diversity and anti-prejudice
    counseling for middle school students.
Achievement High School Student Council June 90-June 94
    Leadership training through the following offices:
    Student Body President 93-94
    Junior Class President 92-93
    Sophomore Class Pres. 91-92
    City of Hope-Internship
    with City Manager Jorge Carrasco   Jan. 93 - June 93

HONORS AND AWARDS:
National Honor Society   1990-94
Outstanding Young Woman of the Year   1994
City of Hope's Top Teen   Feb. 1994
Delegate to Washington Presidential Classroom 1994
Most Outstanding Student Government Member 1990-1994

Complete your résumé on this page.

_____

_____

_____

_____

_____

_____

_____

_____

_____

_____

_____

_____

_____

_____

_____

_____

_____

_____

_____

_____

_____

_____

SAMPLE JOB APPLICATION
XYZ Company

January 1, 1995
Date

File Number _____

Hardworker, Ima
Name (Last)   First   Middle)

100 Academic St., Anytown, U.S.A.
Address   City   Zip Code

809 - 567 - 1234
Telephone Number

Have you ever been employed under a different name? *no*   If yes, what name? _____

PREVIOUS EMPLOYMENT (list most recent experience first) If additional space is needed please attach.
DATES TO/FROM: NAME AND ADDRESS OF EMPLOYER, JOB TITLE AND TYPE OF WORK

1992 - Present   The GAP - Sales Associate
1988 - Present   Church Nursery - Childcare
1988 - 1992   Lawncare (my neighborhood)

EDUCATION

CIRCLE HIGHEST YEAR COMPLETED:

6 7 8 9 10 11 (12) 13 14 15 16   (DIPLOMA)

CURRENTLY ENROLLED IN HIGH SCHOOL COMPLETION COURSE?
COMPLETION DATE: _____

NAME OF SCHOOL & LOCATION: DEGREE   MAJOR   DATE COMPLETED

Achievement High School   *Graduated : 1994*
                                                   GPA : 3.66
Success Middle School   *1988 - 1990*

REFERENCES

List the names of three persons who can give information about your background, character, abilities, etc.

NAME	ADDRESS	RELATIONSHIP TO YOU
Mr. John Jones	*123 Elm St.*	*Teacher*
Ms. Susan Smith	*456 Main St.*	*Employer*

JOB APPLICATION

Date _____

File Number _____

_____
Name (Last   First   Middle)

_____
Address   City   Zip Code

_____
Telephone Number

Have you ever been employed under a different name? _____ If yes, what name? _____

PREVIOUS EMPLOYMENT (list most recent experience first) If additional space is needed please attach.
DATES TO/FROM: NAME AND ADDRESS OF EMPLOYER, JOB TITLE AND TYPE OF WORK

_____

_____

_____

_____

_____

_____

E D U C A T I O N

CIRCLE HIGHEST YEAR COMPLETED: CURRENTLY ENROLLED IN HIGH
                                                  SCHOOL COMPLETION COURSE?
6 7 8 9 10 11 12 13 14 15 16   DIPLOMA   COMPLETION DATE: _____

NAME OF SCHOOL & LOCATION: DEGREE   MAJOR   DATE COMPLETED

_____

_____

_____

_____

R E F E R E N C E S

List the names of three persons who can give information about your background, character, abilities, etc.

NAME   ADDRESS   RELATIONSHIP TO YOU

_____

_____

_____

LESSON SIX — Job Interviews

In the space provided below, script out responses to the following typical interview questions:

I understand you are interested in a position at XYZ Company. Tell me about your qualifications for this position.

_____

_____

_____

_____

Tell me about your work experience.

_____

_____

_____

_____

If I were to ask someone who knew you well what they thought was your best quality, what do you think they would say?

_____

_____

_____

_____

Do you have any questions about our company or the position?

_____

_____

_____

_____

I appreciate your coming in for this interview. I will be making a decision within the next week.

_____

_____

Below list good interviewing techniques you need to remember.

_____

_____

_____

_____

Appropriate dress for an interview would be:

Male: _____

_____

_____

Female: _____

_____

_____

Barriers to employment would be:

_____

_____

_____

_____

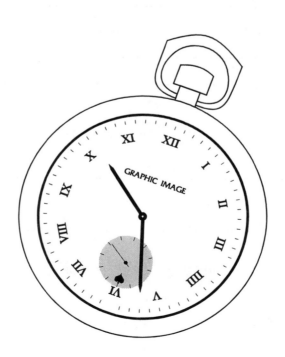

LESSON SEVEN — Training Opportunities for Careers

In the space below write a short paragraph on what you learned from the reports on:

Apprenticeships:

_____

_____

_____

_____

On-The-Job-Training:

_____

_____

_____

_____

Mentoring:

_____

_____

_____

_____

Shadowing:

_____

_____

_____

_____

Internships:

_____

_____

_____

_____

Any other hands-on career exploration opportunities:

_____

_____

_____

_____

_____

_____

_____

_____

_____

_____

_____

_____

CHAPTER ELEVEN — DOLLARS AND SENSE

LESSON ONE — Economic Independence

Write a paragraph on what you learned (including costs) about the subjects listed below.

Insurance: _____

_____

_____

_____

_____

Credit: _____

_____

_____

_____

_____

Investments: _____

_____

_____

_____

_____

Bank accounts (checking and savings): _____

_____

_____

_____

_____

Any additional economic information: _____

_____

_____

_____

_____

LESSON TWO — Public Assistance

There is public assistance in many areas which is meant to subsidize those individuals making less than a certain income. Be sure to find out what level of income would qualify a person for subsidies.

Write a paragraph on what you learned (including costs) about the subjects listed below.

Housing: _____

_____

_____

_____

Health care:_____

_____

_____

_____

Disaster relief: _____

_____

_____

_____

Child care: _____

_____

_____

_____

Any other public assistance that you learned about:

_____

_____

_____

_____

LESSON THREE — Budget

As part of the research for your budget project, make a list of current salaries for your area. You can get this information from the public library, the local employment office and by reading the classified ads. In some cases, you may want to contact local employers to determine their average salaries.

Note: Also record current AFDC rates, Aid For Dependent Children.

_____

_____

_____

_____

_____

_____

_____

_____

_____

_____

_____

_____

_____

_____

_____

_____

_____

_____

_____

_____

Below is a blank budget. Finalize a budget for the family you design and the career you envision, and record it here. Remember to use pencil so you can make changes.

INCOME:

Take home pay $_____

Social Security Benefits $_____

AFDC $_____

Child Support $_____

Investment Income $_____

Other Income $_____

TOTAL INCOME $_____ $_____

EXPENSES: (Monthly costs unless noted otherwise)

HOUSING: Total

    Public Housing: $_____ $_____

    One Bedroom Apartment: $_____ $_____

    Two Bedroom Apartment: $_____ $_____

    Rental House: $_____ $_____

    Purchased House:

        House payment $_____

        Taxes $_____

        Insurance $_____

        Maintenance $_____

        Sub Total $_____ $_____

UTILITIES:

    Electricity $_____

    Gas $_____

    Water $_____

    Garbage $_____

    Sub Total $_____ $_____

TELEPHONE: $_____

CABLE TV: $_____

FOOD COSTS:

    Adult(s) $_____

    Child(ren) $_____

    Sub Total $_____ $_____

CLOTHING:

    Adult(s) $_____

    Child(ren) $_____

    Sub Total $_____ $_____

GROOMING & HYGIENE:

    Adult male $_____

    Adult female $_____

    Child(ren) $_____

    Sub Total $_____ $_____

		Less Government Assistance:	Total:
HEALTH CARE:			
Doctor (per visit)	$_____	$ (_____)	
Dentist (per visit)	$_____	$ (_____)	
Medicine	$_____	$ (_____)	
Health aids	$_____	$ (_____)	
Medical Insurance			
Single adult	$_____	$ (_____)	
Family	$_____	$ (_____)	
Sub Total	$_____	$ (_____)	$_____
CHILD CARE:	$_____	$ (_____)	$_____
TRANSPORTATION:			
Car			
Payment	$_____		
Gas/Maint.	$_____		
Insurance	$_____		
Sub Total			$_____
Public transportation	$_____		$_____
Bicycle			
Payment	$_____		
Maintenance	$_____		
Sub Total			$_____
RECREATION:			
Movies	$_____		
Sports	$_____		
Dances	$_____		
Concerts	$_____		
Other	$_____		
Sub Total			$_____
CHARITABLE CONTRIBUTIONS:			$_____
DEBTS:			
Credit Cards	$_____		
Loan Payments	$_____		
Sub Total			$_____
SAVINGS:			$_____
OTHER:			$_____
TOTAL MONTHLY EXPENSES:			$_____
			_____ x12
TOTAL YEARLY EXPENSES:			$_____

NOTES

BOOK FIVE

Making a Difference

CHAPTER TWELVE — SOCIAL ACTION

LESSON ONE — Politics and Laws

In the space below diagram the organizational chart for your city, state or the federal government.

Briefly state how an ordinance or law is enacted by the governmental structure you depicted above.

_____

_____

_____

_____

_____

_____

_____

_____

_____

_____

_____

_____

LESSON TWO — Leadership

In the space below list the qualities that you feel are important in a leader.

_____

_____

_____

Refer to the sentence you completed in your **Thoughts for Today.** Does the type leader that you are likely to follow have the qualities you listed above? Why do you think this is true or not true?

_____

_____

_____

Select one person that you consider to be a great leader and write a short paragraph on why you chose that person as a leader you admire. This can be a historical figure or a modern day leader. It can be a world leader or a fellow classmate.

_____

_____

_____

_____

_____

_____

_____

_____

_____

_____

LESSON THREE — Choosing an Issue

My *number one* issue is:

_____

_____

_____

Some facts and statistics about my issue are:

_____

_____

_____

_____

_____

_____

_____

_____

_____

_____

_____

_____

_____

_____

_____

_____

_____

_____

_____

LESSON FOUR — Taking Action

Arlene's Ideal Scene for School Ecology

The circle that says I AM stands for you, having experienced your dream come true.

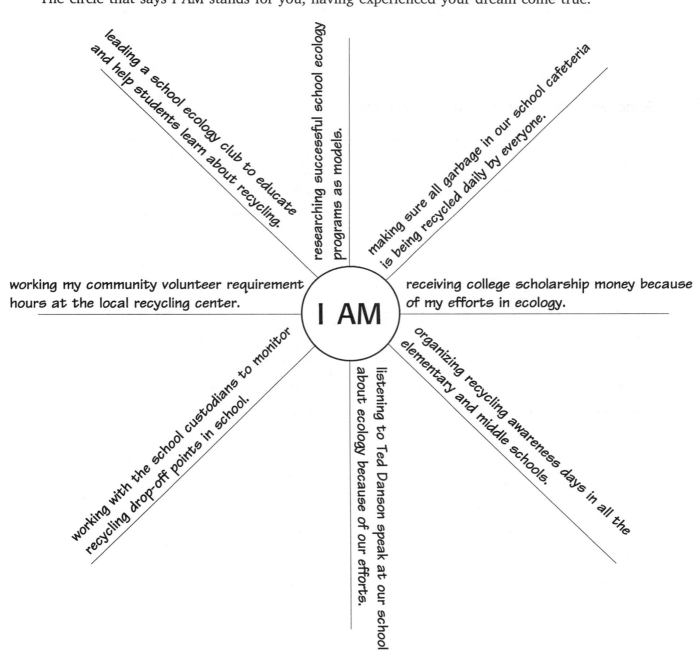

leading a school ecology club to educate and help students learn about recycling.

researching successful school ecology programs as models.

making sure all garbage in our school cafeteria is being recycled daily by everyone.

working my community volunteer requirement hours at the local recycling center.

I AM

receiving college scholarship money because of my efforts in ecology.

working with the school custodians to monitor recycling drop-off points in school.

listening to Ted Danson speak at our school about ecology because of our efforts.

organizing recycling awareness days in all the elementary and middle schools.

This exercise adapted with permission from the University of Santa Monica.

Think ahead six months or a year. Using the I AM as the beginning, write specific active verbs and phrases on the spokes that describe what you are doing in your ideal scene. You may want to look at the example on the previous page for ideas. Allow yourself to dream. At least half of the spokes must be reachable in the time frame, but the other spokes can be "stretches." Place at least eight spokes on your wheel.

_____'s   *Ideal Scene For* _____
Your Name   *Goal*

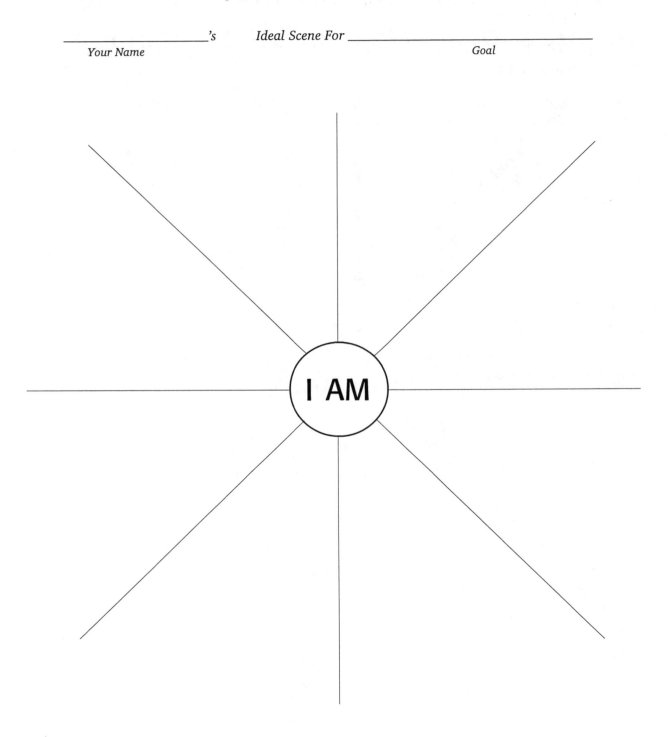

Sample Commitment Statement

I will arrange a meeting with the principal to discuss my ideas for a school recycling program by September 30.

I will approach the student government to organize a school ecology club at the first meeting of the new school year.

I will read the paper daily and clip all articles pertaining to ecology to expand my knowledge about this topic. I will begin today.

My Commitment Statement

1. _____

   _____

2. _____

   _____

3. _____

   _____

Thoughts for Today

_____

_____

_____

_____

_____

_____

_____

_____

_____

_____

_____

_____

_____

_____

_____

_____

_____

_____

_____

_____

_____

_____

_____

_____

_____

Thoughts for Today

Thoughts for Today

Thoughts for Today

Thoughts for Today

Thoughts for Today

_____
_____
_____
_____
_____
_____
_____
_____
_____
_____
_____
_____
_____
_____
_____
_____
_____
_____
_____
_____
_____
_____
_____
_____
_____
_____
_____
_____

Thoughts for Today

Thoughts for Today

_____
_____
_____
_____
_____
_____
_____
_____
_____
_____
_____
_____
_____
_____
_____
_____
_____
_____
_____
_____
_____
_____
_____
_____
_____
_____

Thoughts for Today

_____

_____

_____

_____

_____

_____

_____

_____

_____

_____

_____

_____

_____

_____

_____

_____

_____

_____

_____

_____

_____

_____

_____

_____

_____

_____

_____

Thoughts for Today

_____
_____
_____
_____
_____
_____
_____
_____
_____
_____
_____
_____
_____
_____
_____
_____
_____
_____
_____
_____
_____
_____
_____
_____
_____
_____
_____

Thoughts for Today

Thoughts for Today

_____

_____

_____

_____

_____

_____

_____

_____

_____

_____

_____

_____

_____

_____

_____

_____

_____

_____

_____

_____

_____

_____

_____

_____

_____

_____

Thoughts for Today

Thoughts for Today

Thoughts for Today

Thoughts for Today

Thoughts for Today

_____
_____
_____
_____
_____
_____
_____
_____
_____
_____
_____
_____
_____
_____
_____
_____
_____
_____
_____
_____
_____
_____
_____
_____
_____
_____
_____
_____
_____

Thoughts for Today

Thoughts for Today

_____

_____

_____

_____

_____

_____

_____

_____

_____

_____

_____

_____

_____

_____

_____

_____

_____

_____

_____

_____

_____

_____

_____

_____

_____

_____

_____

_____

_____

_____

_____

_____

Thoughts for Today

Thoughts for Today

_____
_____
_____
_____
_____
_____
_____
_____
_____
_____
_____
_____
_____
_____
_____
_____
_____
_____
_____
_____
_____
_____
_____
_____
_____
_____

Thoughts for Today

Skill Box

_____

_____

_____

_____

_____

_____

_____

_____

_____

_____

_____

_____

_____

_____

_____

_____

_____

_____

_____

_____

_____

_____

_____

_____

_____

_____

_____

_____

_____

Skill Box

_____
_____
_____
_____
_____
_____
_____
_____
_____
_____
_____
_____
_____
_____
_____
_____
_____
_____
_____
_____
_____
_____
_____
_____
_____
_____
_____

Skill Box

_____

_____

_____

_____

_____

_____

_____

_____

_____

_____

_____

_____

_____

_____

_____

_____

_____

_____

_____

_____

_____

_____

_____

_____

_____

_____

_____

Skill Box

_____
_____
_____
_____
_____
_____
_____
_____
_____
_____
_____
_____
_____
_____
_____
_____
_____
_____
_____
_____
_____
_____
_____
_____
_____
_____
_____
_____
_____

Skill Box

_____
_____
_____
_____
_____
_____
_____
_____
_____
_____
_____
_____
_____
_____
_____
_____
_____
_____
_____
_____
_____
_____
_____
_____
_____
_____
_____
_____
_____
_____

Skill Box

_____

_____

_____

_____

_____

_____

_____

_____

_____

_____

_____

_____

_____

_____

_____

_____

_____

_____

_____

_____

_____

_____

_____

_____

_____

_____

_____

Skill Box

_____

_____

_____

_____

_____

_____

_____

_____

_____

_____

_____

_____

_____

_____

_____

_____

_____

_____

_____

_____

_____

_____

_____

_____

_____

_____

_____

Skill Box

Skill Box

_____
_____
_____
_____
_____
_____
_____
_____
_____
_____
_____
_____
_____
_____
_____
_____
_____
_____
_____
_____
_____
_____
_____
_____
_____
_____
_____
_____
_____
_____
_____
_____

Skill Box

_____

_____

_____

_____

_____

_____

_____

_____

_____

_____

_____

_____

_____

_____

_____

_____

_____

_____

_____

_____

_____

_____

_____

_____

_____

_____

_____

_____

Skill Box

_____

_____

_____

_____

_____

_____

_____

_____

_____

_____

_____

_____

_____

_____

_____

_____

_____

_____

_____

_____

_____

_____

_____

_____

_____

_____

_____

Skill Box

_____
_____
_____
_____
_____
_____
_____
_____
_____
_____
_____
_____
_____
_____
_____
_____
_____
_____
_____
_____
_____
_____
_____
_____
_____
_____
_____
_____
_____
_____

Skill Box

_____
_____
_____
_____
_____
_____
_____
_____
_____
_____
_____
_____
_____
_____
_____
_____
_____
_____
_____
_____
_____
_____
_____
_____
_____
_____
_____

Skill Box

_____

_____

_____

_____

_____

_____

_____

_____

_____

_____

_____

_____

_____

_____

_____

_____

_____

_____

_____

_____

_____

_____

_____

_____

_____

_____

_____

_____

_____

Skill Box

_____

_____

_____

_____

_____

_____

_____

_____

_____

_____

_____

_____

_____

_____

_____

_____

_____

_____

_____

_____

_____

_____

_____

_____

_____

_____

_____

_____

ACKNOWLEDGMENTS

The creator of *MAKING CHOICES: Life Skills for Adolescents*, is Girls Incorporated of Greater Santa Barbara, a non-profit organization which provides program services for young people, ages five through seventeen. Our mission is to reach youth throughout the country by developing and delivering programs and materials which promote gender equality and self-sufficiency.

Mary H. Halter is former executive director of Girls Club of Scottsdale, AZ, and currently provides sex education training for Girls Incorporated on the national level. She works part-time as a health educator for Phoenix Girls and Boys Clubs, specializing in HIV and sex education. She provides training for youth who are incarcerated in the Arizona Department of Youth Treatment and Rehabilitation. She provides consultation and training throughout the country for those who teach and lead youth in schools, non-profit organizations and juvenile institutions. Mary is the mother of four adult children.

Barbara Fierro Lang is executive director of Girls Incorporated of Greater Santa Barbara, CA, and former executive director of Girls Incorporated of Rapid City, SD. She also served as executive director of Big Brothers and Big Sisters of the Black Hills (SD). Her involvement with Girls Incorporated extends over twenty-five years. She has served on the national board of directors of Girls Incorporated and is one of the architects of Girls Incorporated's core program and philosophy. Barbara is a national trainer for Girls Incorporated. She is the mother of five grown children.

Girls Incorporated of Greater Santa Barbara is extremely grateful to these two women for giving countless hours of dedicated service to this project.

We are eminently beholden to Barbara Greene and Fred Klein each of whom dedicated many long hours to the editing process. Barbara has been a copy editor for nearly every publication produced by Advocacy Press over the past ten years. She does her job well. Fred Klein, a former editor for Doubleday Dell, is a volunteer who gives freely of his time and talent both as an editor and as a member of the Advocacy Press Committee.

We devote our undying admiration and gratitude to our illustrator, Itoko Maeno, who brings our work to life with her wonderful images. We are blessed with the talent of Chris Nolt, our book designer and typesetter whose dedication and hard work is always above and beyond the call of duty.

Special appreciation is extended to Oshi Jauco Owens, Arlene Stepputat and Jo Gottfried, exceptional employees of Girls Incorporated, who contributed their ideas to the Curriculum Guide.

Notable thanks go to the group of educators and youth leaders who attended our initial training and gave us their professional feedback before the final revision of the Curriculum Guide.

Jonathan Haley deserves a special note of thanks for his contributions to the Friday Forum.

Our highest respect goes to Senator Diane Watson, Dr. Inez Hope, Milton Wilson and the California Legislature for dedicating their time and talents to the introduction, passing and fulfillment of SB 1307/SB 324 which is the impetus for the development of this work.

And, finally, to the children of the world. We are grateful you are here. We trust you to become the parents, the workers and the leaders of our nations. We dedicate this work to you:

Learn much, enjoy your life,
Travel all roads with confidence.
Things may happen that you cannot control,
But you can control the way you act when they happen.
Your readiness for today decides your success for tomorrow.